Arthur D Atkinson
Aug 69
from Allen.

Sermons From Paul

VOLUME II in the TRUETT MEMORIAL SERIES

SERMONS FROM PAUL

by

GEORGE W. TRUETT, D.D., LL.D.

Edited by
Powhatan W. James, Th.D., D.D.

WM. B. EERDMANS PUBLISHING COMPANY

GRAND RAPIDS   1947   MICHIGAN

Sermons from Paul
by George W. Truett, D.D. LL.D

———

Copyright 1947, *by*
Wm. B. Eerdmans Publishing Company

Set up and printed, 1947
First Printing, March, 1947

PRINTED IN THE UNITED STATES OF AMERICA

DEDICATION

This and other volumes
of sermons and addresses
in this series by Dr. George W. Truett
are dedicated to
his beloved
First Baptist Church, Dallas, Texas
where most of them
were delivered

FOREWORD

BECAUSE Dr. George W. Truett was such an ardent admirer of Paul, the Apostle to the Gentiles, and delighted to quote him and to preach on Pauline texts, it has been thought fitting to devote Volume II of *The Truett Memorial Series* to sermons based on the writings of Paul. Dr. Truett never wearied of saying, "Paul was the greatest single credential of Christianity since Christ ascended from the Mount of Olives."

The compiler and editor of this series of sermons by Dr. Truett is deeply indebted to Dr. T. L. Holcomb, executive secretary of the Sunday School Board of the Southern Baptist Convention, Nashville, Tennessee, for permission to reprint two sermons appearing in volumes whose copyright is now owned by that Board. These sermons are: "A Religion That Is Divine," from *A Quest for Souls*, and "A Prayer for Patience," from *Follow Thou Me*. Similar permission was graciously given by the Fleming H. Revell Company, New York City, as to "Trumpeting the Gospel," from *We Would See Jesus*.

Volume I of this series, *Some Vital Questions*, was received so cordially by reviewers and the general public that we feel greatly encouraged to press on with the privileged task of compiling, editing and publishing this second volume and the others yet to follow.

POWHATAN W. JAMES

PRESIDENT'S OFFICE
BETHEL WOMAN'S COLLEGE
HOPKINSVILLE, KENTUCKY

CONTENTS

Foreword... 7

1. What We Preach... 11
   A Convention Sermon

2. The Adequacy of Christ.. 33

3. Why Christ Died... 47

4. A Religion That Is Divine.. 57

5. Think on These Things.. 73

6. Permanent Profit... 85

7. The Secret of Contentment...................................... 97

8. A Prayer for Patience...111

9. A Living Sacrifice..123

10. The Christian Optimist...139

11. Stir Up the Gift of God...153

12. Trumpeting the Gospel...167

13. Are You Ready? 187

14. Christian Assurance...201

SERMON I

What We Preach

S E R M O N   I

What We Preach

<hr />

*For we preach not ourselves, but
Christ Jesus the Lord; and ourselves your servants for Jesus'
sake.*   II CORINTHIANS 4:5

BROTHER PRESIDENT and my dear fellow-
workers of this Convention:

I would be allowed the privilege for a moment before coming to the text to say that I have a very deep sense of the
marked courtesy that is done to any man who is asked to
preach its Convention Sermon. Quite well do I understand
that there is no more reason for my preaching this sermon
than for any one of hundreds of my cherished fellow preachers who are in this Convention hall today, or who are scattered
throughout this great State. Indeed, there are hundreds of
God's preachers in this land whose voices are rarely ever
heard in the sessions of a Convention, at whose feet this
Convention would delight to sit to hear them tell about
Jesus. I would cast myself upon your most brotherly sympathy
and I would beseech you to help me today by your prayers.

Probably the most glorious week that our Baptist people
ever have in this State is that week in which comes their
annual Convention with its auxiliary meetings. What is said
and done here to a remarkable degree sets the pace for our
fellow-workers throughout all our broad land. Oh, what
need of humility and heart-searchings when we come to the
Convention! What need of the prayers for the light and
leading of the Divine Spirit!

The text is in Paul's Second Letter to the Corinthians, fourth chapter and fifth verse: "For we preach not ourselves, but Christ Jesus the Lord; and ourselves your servants for Jesus' sake."

The most glorious exponent of the gospel ministry that this world has ever seen was the Apostle Paul. He is the highest product of Christianity, he is the greatest single personal credential that Christ's Gospel has ever produced. Long before Wesley said, "The world is my parish," Paul had made the world *his* parish. The greatest man that ever sailed the Mediterranean Sea was not Pericles, nor Alexander, nor Hannibal, nor Caesar, but the plain preacher Paul. He did the most gigantic missionary work that the ages have ever known when he became Christ's preacher; from that hour he gladly faced innumerable difficulties and braved untold hardships and suffering, all because of his devotion to the Lord Jesus Christ.

Verily Paul "magnified the ministry." The most important work in all the world is the work of the pulpit. There can be no substitute for the spoken word from a living pulpit. "It pleased God by the foolishness of preaching to save them that believe." Whatever the progress and triumphs of the schools and of civilization, with all its multiform organizations, there can never be any displacement of the work of the prophets of God. The halcyon days of Christianity have always been the days of the right kind of preaching. All the decadent days of Christianity have been the days of the wrong kind of preaching. The Christian pulpit cannot be what it ought to be, and what God designs, if it be without the right kind of men in the pulpit. The pulpit is not the place for men of anemic spirit; they had better stay out of it. It is not the place for prigs and fops and dandies and for men seeking selfish ends. The most robust and virile and masculine and heroic business that earth ever saw is the right kind of preaching. Life is epic with the true preacher. The preacher, first of all, must be a genuine man. Paul was that. John the

Baptist was that. They tell us that "knowledge is power," and so it is, but character is far more so. It was the secret that explained Washington, Gladstone and Pitt. What a preacher is within himself counts far more than what he says. Phillips Brooks' definition of preaching is: "Truth plus personality"; and another great definition: "A great life telling a great truth." A little man cannot be a great preacher. It is a crime for any preacher to be a little man, to be petty and ungenerous and envious and self-seeking and mean. Kingdoms call for kings to rule them; a king is a man who can; empires call for emperors. The greatest message ever given to mortals calls for the right kind of messengers!

In this chapter from which the text is taken Paul gives us certain suggestions of vital qualities that ought to be regnant in the minister of Christ's gospel. They are summoned to courageous endurance: "Seeing that we have this ministry, we faint not." Courage is a qualification never to be lost sight of by God's prophet and preacher. The preacher is called to courageous endurance.

My personal belief is that no lazy man should ever be a preacher. The most indefatigable toiler the earth ever saw should be God's divinely appointed preacher and prophet. If his people believe him lazy, he is vitally shorn of his power. "Cursed is every one that doeth the work of the Lord negligently." The naturalists tells us that nature denies beauty to every lazy animal. The ugliest biped in the world is a lazy preacher. The true preacher is a man of purity, "renouncing the hidden things of shame." He is to be an example to the believer in works, in manner of life, in faith, in word, in purity. They that bear the vessels of the Lord must be clean men. Oh, the grief that the preacher, careless about his habits and example and his reputation and influence, brings to all serious men!

The right kind of preacher is a man of marked integrity. Paul describes him as "one not walking in ways of craftiness; one not handling the word of God deceitfully." The fundamental virtue for the preacher and for everybody else is sincerity. It is unpardonable for God's preacher not to be honest and genuine to the very center of his being. Life is a ghastly lie if the preacher is not sincere. I would as soon hear the Gospel from the lips of a drunkard as from a man who would tell a lie. Oh, my brothers, in this incomparable work of the Christian ministry, whatever else we may or may not be, let us by the grace of God, be the right kind of men.

Now in Paul's great text here, he sets forth the message and the mission and the motive in all Christian service: "For we preach not ourselves, but Christ Jesus the Lord; and ourselves your servants for Jesus' sake." The subject matter of all true preaching is stated there.

"We preach not ourselves, but Christ Jesus the Lord." Paul states it for us first negatively. "We preach not ourselves." He makes a disclaimer to start with. It is very easy for a preacher to preach himself, but that is very bad homiletics and very bad religion. A preacher preaches himself when he preaches his own vagaries, speculations, or opinions, or mere theories, or doubts. Christ's pulpit is no place for the spiritual stammerer. "I believe, therefore have I spoken." "We can but speak the things we have seen and heard."

A preacher preaches himself oftentimes by absurd methods and reverence-debauching themes. Take this list, culled from a recent series:

> "Can a Man Love Twice?"
> "Autumn Leaves"
> "Going up Salt River"
> "Skinning the Major"
> "Saul Seeking His Father's Asses"

"Tell it not in Gath, publish it not in the streets of Askalon" —a prophet of God out in the race with little cheap theatricals! If I could get the ear and heart of the young man beginning his ministry today, I would beseech him to shun—as

16

he would shun the deadly poison—every tendency within him, every urge his heart feels for fame, popularity, and publicity in the ministry. Fame is nothing, publicity is nothing, popularity is nothng; doing the will of God modestly and faithfully is everything, and the record of it is kept on high. Most of the best work done in this world by preachers has been done, and is being done, by men back there in the quiet nooks, whose names never one time get into the papers. The world's great preachers cannot be guilty of the folly I have just depicted. Imagine B. H. Carroll giving a series of sermons on the themes I have named. Imagine Spurgeon, or Alexander Maclaren, or Phillips Brooks, or John A. Broadus, or any of the princes of the Christian pulpit giving such a series! Paul preached "Christ Jesus the Lord." If the mighty Apostle had that incomparable method, surely his brothers, lesser and weaker, need to walk in his steps. It will ever be true, my brothers, that the world's cry in its sin, shall be this: "Sir, we would see Jesus." And it will ever be true that the chief magnet to draw wearied, sinning men out of the sloughs, darkness, death and doom is this: "And I, if I be lifted up from the earth, will draw all men unto Me."

Paul states his case positively. "We preach not ourselves, but we preach Christ Jesus the Lord." That collocation of names is not accidental; it is deeply significant: "Christ Jesus the Lord." We preach Jesus; not merely His humanity. We delight in His humanity, His perfect humanity; we love to think of Him as a babe on his mother's heart, to think of Him as a lad asking and answering questions in the Temple at twelve, to think of Him glorifying toil the world round and through the ages, to think of Him as brother; but if Jesus was only human, wehave no Gospel at all. They placarded the walls of the public buildings in France years ago with the question: "Can faith in a dead man save you?" Not at all. We do not preach faith in a dead man; we preach faith in one who conquered death and brought life and immortality to light through His gospel. Jesus Christ is our

17

message. We preach Jesus Christ, the anointed Messiah, the God-appointed Deliverer, the divinely-sent Saviour. Jesus was more than a perfect example.

You delight to think of one who walked the world without a taint of sin, but you and I should be in despair today if we had only the blameless example of Jesus. Jesus is the world's perfect teacher, but that is not enough. Yonder at Caesarea Philippi He asked His apostles, when He had them apart: "Whom do men say that I am?" They answered: "Some say John the Baptist; some Elijah; and others, Jeremiah, or one of the prophets." And then He came closer: "Whom do you say that I am?" Simon Peter made prompt reply: "Thou art the Christ." Then He made the glad response: "On this rock I will build My church, and the gates of hell shall not prevail against it." You cannot build a church of Christ apart from His deity. A church mocking the deity of Christ is no more a scriptural church than is a grocery store on yonder street. Christ is God manifest in the flesh, God fore-shortened, making atonement for human sin. This is the world's hope. How the name Jesus takes on the meaning of infinite preciousness! "Thou shalt call His name Jesus, for He shall save His people from their sins." In the thought of God, man has only one enemy and that enemy is sin. This earth would be fair as the island valley of the Avalon if no sin were here. Why did the Lord Jesus come down from heaven among men? He was manifested to take away our sins; He was manifested that He might destroy the works of the devil. "Behold the Lamb of God that taketh away the sin of the world." "The Son of Man is come to seek and to save the lost." "And now, once in the end of the world, He hath appeared to put away sin by the sacrifice of Himself." Jesus is the world's Saviour because of His essential humanity and His essential deity. And now His name takes on a meaning sweeter than the music from any Aeolian harp:

> Sweetest note in seraph song,
> Sweetest name on mortal tongue;
> Sweetest carol ever sung,
>> Jesus, Blessed Jesus.

That is the name that heals like a medicine and soothes like anodyne; that is the name that quiets our fears, relieves our agonies and dispels our despair. That is the name that transfigures common men and women and sends them out to be the world's heroes and heroines. That is the name which the dear lips that are silent first taught us, when as prattling babes we all lay on our mother's heart, a name sweeter than even mother's name; and that is the name which, I trust, will be last on our lips before they are hushed into their last silence.

> Jesus the name that calms our fears,
>> That bids our sorrows cease;
> 'Tis music in the sinner's ears,
>> And life and joy and peace.

Since Jesus is the divine Saviour, we gladly go with His gospel to all the world and commend His grace and love to sinners everywhere. There are no incurables in the sight of Jesus. Sin is the one unbearable yoke of the world. It is the one ghastly tragedy, and certain cults about us are failing and must fail utterly because they deny the fact of sin. Their message has no power to loosen the slave and disenthrall those who are chained, but we have a gospel which can deliver from sin. The Bible does not paint in glowing colors the condition of men. It portrays sin in all his hideous and ghastly aspects, but it says: "Where sin abounded, grace did much more abound"; and with that gospel we can go to earth's remotest bounds and tell sinners everywhere that they need not despair.

Certain ethnologists, sociologists, moralists, and others talk to us about submerged and helpless classes, but with this divine Saviour, you cannot write Dante's word: "Let all who enter here abandon hope." Jesus Christ came into the world to save sinners, even the chief of sinners. Although one's sins be as scarlet, that divine Saviour will make them as white as snow. Spurgeon said: "You can unlock the very chambers of hell; even the vilest sinner, if he will come to Jesus repentant of sin, that divine Saviour will absolve him from all sin."

Edward Irving tells us that he once went out to see a young man who was dying in an attic, a boy notorious for his sin. Others had talked to him but seemed to make no impression. Presently Irving bent over him and touched his forehead and said to him: "God loves you enough to die for you"; and he opened his eyes in staring wonder and said: "Does He? Then I will love Him back." And the boy went out of that place of squalor and wretchedness and doom up to the starry heights, clinging to Christ. This is our gospel—a divine Saviour, and with that gospel we will go to men the world round and tell them they need not die eternally.

But that is not all. "We preach Jesus as Lord." The supreme need for every human being is to have a Lord, to have a Master; men are made to obey. You say that man was made to be free, and so he was. Equally so, man was made to obey, and all is chaos in that human life which does not have the right kind of a Master, even Christ Jesus, the Lord. The Lordship of Christ is the basis for all our contentions. You ask us why we insist forever on believers' baptism, and that baptism a burial. We cite you back, without a word of controversy, to the Lordship of Christ. You ask us why we give our money and give our lives to making the name of Jesus known all around the world; we point you back to the Lordship of Christ. There is the blessedness that goes with education and with civilization in all its triumphs; there is a glory that attaches to chivalry, when chivalry cares for a woman, but passing by all these as superficial as compared with the other, we answer: "We are missionaries, from here to the ends of the earth, because our risen and glorified Lord said, 'All authority is given unto me in heaven and on earth; go ye therefore unto all the world and preach the gospel to every creature.'" There is our basis for missions and, whenever we get away from that, the nerve of missions is cut and paralyzed.

The Lordship of Christ involves some vital corollaries. For one thing, the human soul must be free to make its own approach to that divine Saviour. Personality in religion must ever be inscribed on all our banners; one must believe for himself, and repent for himself, and be baptized for himself, and pray for himself, and give for himself. The Lordship of the Christ involves the great doctrine that religion and the State must be utterly divorced and separate. "My kingdom is not of this world," said Jesus. The Pharisees came to Him one day and asked Him if it was lawful to pay tribute unto Caesar. He took their coin, which had on it the image and superscription of Caesar, and made the telling answer: "Render unto Caesar the things that are Caesar's and unto God the things that are God's." In that sentence Jesus stated an aphorism of immeasurable wisdom. That significant statement started a new era for all the world. That sentence was the sunrise gun of a new day for humanity. When Caesar interferes with religion, he always makes a muddle of it. The age-long contention of our fathers has been that the human soul must be free. There must be no restraint nor constraint upon such soul in the matter of religion. No institution, whether Church or State, and no person—whether parent or preacher, or pope, or priest—must dare to come between that soul and its divine Lord. This is the crowning jewel of humanity—the freedom of the human soul in its approach unto the exalted Lord. Our fathers have made this age-long contention all down the centuries. A true Baptist could not persecute others. If anywhere you find so-called Baptists persecuting Protestants or Catholics, Gentile or Jew, pagan, heathen, sinner, or anybody else, they are belying the age-long contention of our people. Our fathers through the centuries have held to this great doctrine, even with the shedding of their blood. Every land on the continent of Europe has been stained by their blood because of their fealty to this principle. Yonder in one of the colonies, there is blood on the whipping post for our contention for this principle. Our plain Baptist preachers on both sides of the sea have said: "We prefer to lie in jails rather than take license from the civil governments to preach Christ's spiritual gospel." *Let Caesar's dues be paid to Caesar and his throne, but consciences and souls were made for God, for the Lord, alone.*

The Lordship of Christ is a supreme necessity for every human being. The great Doctor Wilkinson's aphorism is a true one, that our contention is based upon obedience to Christ, the governing principle in the kingdom of Christ. Obedience is vital in the home, and in the school, and in the army. In religion man must have a master, and the exalted Saviour once offered, by the sacrifice of Himself, to make atonement for human sin, stands before men as such Master. The supreme necessity for all human hearts is to have such a Master. Every great heart in its serious hour recognizes such vital need.

Huxley, the great modern scientific man, said one day: "If there could come unto me some power, wound up like a clock, so that from that day on I would say the right words, have the right thoughts, and do the right deeds, I would close up with that power." We would say to Mr. Huxley: "Mr. Huxley and your fellow scientists, Jesus is that power, better than all the clocks of the earth." In the hour of temptation, I need somebody to help me; when the scorching fires burn me with their awful suggestiveness; when the hour of darkness comes I need somebody to be a light to me; in the hour of weakness, I need somebody to give me superhuman strength; in the hour of grief, when the very stars are hidden and I hear no voice of comfort, I need somebody with divine power, on whose bosom I can lean, as John leaned on Christ at the supper. Jesus is that Somebody.

The great Martin Luther sat there by his little Margaret, four years old and dearer to her father than his own heart's blood. He prayed that her life might be spared. The intrepid man did not see how he could go on without little Margaret. The doctor touched the father lightly on the shoulder and said: "Mr. Luther, little Margaret is going now." The heart of the great reformer-preacher was almost broken and he said: "Is it possible that my sweet child can go into the darkness and cold by herself?" Then, in a moment more, he said: "No! 'Yea, though I walk through the valley of the shadow of death, I will fear no evil; for Thou are with me'!" "Christ hath abolished death and brought life and immortality to light through His gospel." The substance of His words to John on Patmos was this: "Fear not, I am alive; I was dead; I am alive now and hold in my hands the keys of death and the invisible world, and I am alive forevermore." I saw a wife a little while ago standing beside the bier of her husband. They sang, "How Firm a Foundation," and when they came to the second stanza:

"In every condition, in sickness, in health,"

she joined in. She whispered to me when the song was done: "I could sing it because Christ has me in His keeping forevermore."

When we take up our tasks and duties, our supreme need is a divine Master. At the battle of Sedan, King William heard that one of his bravest officers was mortally wounded. He hastened to the dying officer, and bent over the brave young fellow and said with deep emotion: "My boy, is all well?" With a smile on his face, he answered back: "All is well where you lead." Well may we say: "King Jesus, lead on! Thou art our Master. All is well."

But Paul also utters a great truth for Christs' workers in this same great text: "We preach not ourselves, but Christ Jesus the Lord; and ourselves your servants." Great are the implications of this statement by Paul. The obligation and meaning of every cross in the world is service. The meaning of every Christian gift and grace is service; the meaning of all education and wealth, and of every other power with which Christianity is dowered, is service in behalf of needy humanity. Service is the divine Master's test for His people. "By their fruits ye shall know them." A creed is a great thing provided the creed issues in great deeds. The ideal life was stated in five little words: "He went about doing good." You cannot add to that. When you and I in our little earthly sphere want to walk in the footsteps of the Master we must simply go about doing good. What the world needs is service. Its wounds cannot be staunched by talk; its ignorance cannot be dispelled by talk; its sufferings cannot be relieved by talk; its sins cannot be cured by mere talk. The world needs service; only in this way, my comrades in the great work, can Christ's people authenticate their faith. "Why call ye Me, Lord, Lord, and do not the things which I say?" Faith is more than any mere dogmatism; faith is passion, faith lifts, faith rises, faith achieves; faith is valuable only in proportion as it issues in service. Without service our faith is all dead. Great believers have always been great doers: witness the Apostle Paul; witness Martin Luther; witness B. H. Carroll.

Garibaldi, yonder in Rome in prison, managed to scribble on a little piece of paper and get it back to his soldiers: "If fifty Garibaldi's be thrown into prison, let Rome be free." A passion like that burns like fire and will conquer everything before it. The teaching of Jesus, our Master, is revolutionary as to the supreme things. He never gave a little answer to a big question. One day He was asked, "Who is my neighbor?" And He gave the answer, "Whoever needs you." The meaning of responsibility has not yet been fully disclosed to this great sinning world of ours. Whoever needs me, whether he lives in Texas or in Belgium, or in darkest Africa, or in Japan, he is my neighbor. You ask what is my parish; how many people are in my parish? About two billion people now live in my parish.

Debtorship is our great call. I am a debtor to all men, said the earth's chiefest exponent of religion, debtor to the last limit of my power. We are to say to Lady Bountiful: "Dear woman, put aside the little troubles of life and live on that high plane to which you are called by your divine Lord." We are to say to the princely banker, to the merchant, and to the business man, "Sir, your money is given you for the express business of bringing the world to Christ's feet." We are to say to the scholar, whether man or woman, "Your education is not for personal self-gratification, but it is to be used for winning the world to Christ."

Our task is outlined for us by our risen Lord, and this Convention has addressed itself to that task as unfolded in the three-fold program set for it by our Lord.

First of all, we are to make disciples; we are to go everywhere making disciples. The right kind of evangelism must be proclaimed by us forevermore; that kind of evangelism goes to the very fountain-head of Christianity; that kind of evangelism is part of our religion, just as the fields, mines and forests are a part of our commerce; that kind of evangelism is necessary to the growth of our churches. "Conquest," said Napoleon, "has made me and conquest must maintain me." The drive-wheel for every true church is the right kind of evangelism. It is necessary to the very life of our churches. It is a life and death conquest for us, and in our great business the first behest of discipleship for Christ's church centers on this same evangelism. The churches of the Lord Jesus Christ are the divinely commissioned agents in the vital business of evangelism. They are faithless to their trust and recreant to their highest duty if they fail to major on true evangelism. That kind of evangelism will rid our churches of numerous ills which are prone to invade their ranks and cripple their effectiveness. It is a wholesome tonic, a refreshing shower, a cleansing stream. They tell us in the old myth about the Augean stables that, so long as they took wheelbarrows and spades to cart away the filth, they were

25

never victorious; but one day the river was turned through the Augean stables and all their foulness was washed away. Evangelism is our life-giving river. As Dagon fell when the Philistines brought the Ark of the Lord into their temple at Ashdod, even so will many an evil and idolatrous thing be smashed to bits when the ark of evangelism is established in the churches of our Lord.

> Give us a watchword for the heart,
>   A word of thrilling power;
> A bugle call; a flaming breath,
> That calls to conquest or to death.
> That call comes to us from the skies;
> We must, we must evangelize.

And then we must give ourselves to the great and glorious task of Christian Education — Christian education in fact, Christian education in form, Christian education in reality. If a boy or girl goes out from one of our Christian homes to one of our Christian schools, and meets an atmosphere there in which such child shall come back home a scoffing infidel, somebody has blundered, and every teacher and officer of that institution ought to be on his face before God. Christian schools should have teachers who go to prayer-meeting, and who yearn over the souls of our boys and girls with the passion of a shepherd hunting for the sheep that is lost. We shall gladly and generously give our money to build and strengthen our denominational schools so long as they impart the right kind of education.

Along with that education in the school, there must be the scattering of positive, constructive, healing and life-giving literature. Our religious papers must be fortified, and our tracts, healing and positive, explanatory and constructive, must be scattered through the land like leaves in the valley of Vallambrosa.

Nor is this all. When Jesus sent forth the Apostles, He gave them four imperative tasks: "Heal the sick, cleanse the lepers, raise the dead, and cast out devils." He sends us forth on the same tasks. We have grounds for rejoicing that we are making notable progress in the performance of these tasks through our hospitals, our schools, our orphanages, our evangelism and our mission programs. Our Lord has given us great tasks for which we should be grateful because great tasks help to make a great people. God forbid that we should fumble at a task so world-wide as ours.

When William Carey arose in the little assembly at Kettering in England, he made that assembly epoch-making because on that day he launched forth on the superhuman but divinely appointed program of World Missions. On that day he helped to usher in a new era in the progress of the Kingdom of God.

There is another word: "We preach not ourselves, but Christ Jesus the Lord; and ourselves your servants for Jesus' sake." Motive oxygenizes every quality in human life. What makes life brighter is the presence of a worthy motive; and what makes life dreary is want of a masterful and worthy motive. Christ and Christ alone can give that motive. There is the motive of egoism, which begins and ends with self. Such motive is doomed. The nation that begins and ends with self is doomed. Let this nation, standing now in the most responsible position of all the nations of the earth, forget her high mission and she is doomed. Kipling's *Recessional* is the word for this nation:

> God of our fathers, known of old,
>   Lord of our far-flung battle line,
> Beneath whose awful hand we hold
>   Dominion over palm and pine,
> Lord God of Hosts, be with us yet,
> Lest we forget — lest we forget!
>
> The tumult and the shouting dies,
>   The captains and the kings depart,
> Still stands Thine ancient sacrifice,
>   A humble and a contrite heart.
> Lord God of Hosts, be with us yet,
> Lest we forget — lest we forget!

Far called, our navies melt away,
  On dune and headland sinks the fire,
Lo, all our pomp of yesterday
  Is one with Nineveh and Tyre!
Judge of the nations, spare us yet,
Lest we forget — lest we forget!

If, drunk with sight of power, we loose
  Wild tongues that have not Thee in awe,
Such boastings as the Gentiles use,
  Or lesser breeds without the law,
Lord God of Hosts, be with us yet,
Lest we forget — lest we forget!

For heathen heart that puts her trust
  In reeking tube and iron shard,
All valiant dust that builds on dust,
  And guarding calls not Thee to guard,
For frantic boast and foolish word,
Thy mercy on Thy people, Lord!

A church is doomed that begins and ends with self. Witness the Seven Churches of Asia. The man is doomed who uses his power exclusively for selfish ends. My brothers, there is only one motive sufficient for our task—that motive is love for Christ and His cause. Let any little life become linked in love with Jesus until the earthly day is done, and the gates will be lifted up and the everlasting doors will swing ajar with welcome when such little saint gets home.

Oh, men and women, I come to ask if we will dare to live Christ's religion like it ought to be lived? When Christ calls, "Follow Me," it is not easy to obey. That means death to self, self-will, self-preference; that means a constant crucifixion of self. But, my brothers, no cheap religion is going to win this world. Surely, we should behave ourselves with wisdom from God. Lay the truth to heart now: that no cheap religion is going to bring this world to the feet of God. We must be supremely, utterly dedicated to the will of Christ if we are to win the world to the saving knowledge of God. When they asked Quentin Hogg, that great founder of Polytechnic Institute in London, "How much did it cost to build it, Mr.

Hogg?" he made the modest answer: "Oh, not much, simply one man's life blood."

Men and women, redeemed by Him who poured out His life in atoning sacrifice for us, the only way to win Texas and the world is for us to live our religion with the passion of Christ. The re-birth of spiritual passion is the world's great need now. When John Clifford, the Nonconformist leader in England, was in this country some years ago, he told us about a missionary from India who pleaded with the students in a great English university for volunteers. He wanted six men to go with him; some to teach, some to be doctors, and some to preach. He reminded them that out there they would find every convenience of the home land, golf links, swimming, etc., and the men gave him the icy stare. The great old preacher told us that the next week there came a man from far-off Persia, barely forty years old, with hair as white as snow, who said to the same men: "I want a half dozen men to go back with me. I am nearly to the end; I will promise you an early death; you will not live out half your days; you will go to your graves early. But for Christ's sake, who gave Himself for you, who will be willing to go?" And six stalwart men said they were willing to go on a mission like that. We need a rebirth of the passion of Christ or the world is doomed. The early Christians in a generation shook the Roman Empire. How did they overcome? They overcame by the blood of the Lamb, by the word of their testimony, and they loved not their lives, even unto death.

Oh, brothers, will we dare to be Christians now? The world never saw such an hour as this. In this eventful hour of the ages, we stand at the crossroads of history. Which road will we take? One road is clearly marked: "The Way of Christ." It is the way of righteousness and truth and sacrifice and service. There are blood stains along that way, left there by the Saviour's wounded feet, left there by the martyrs who loved their Lord more than they loved their own lives. The horrible maelstrom of war now engulfing all of Europe, will, no doubt

29

sooner or later, suck us into its frightful vortex of destruction and death. Desperately Europe and the rest of the world will be needing as never before the loftiest exhibition of Christian principles and practices of which the Christian people in these United States are capable. Are we equal to the challenge and opportunities now presented to us as Christians? Can we measure up to the times in which we live? We can, only as Christ shall strengthen and empower and master us. That He will do, provided we dare to yield ourselves fully and unreservedly unto Him who is the King of kings and the Lord of lords, the all-sufficient and all-powerful Saviour.

As we run our race we are cheered on by a great cloud of witnesses. Some of them are looking on from the heavenly heights and others, still in the flesh, intently observe us from the earthly side-lines. Some of these living witnesses are in Waco, some in China and other parts of the world. They are saying: "We are giving our lives, our all, to the King and His kingdom. Won't you reinforce us with your prayers, your money, your very lives?"

A boy in college went away to see his blind father die; there was a great game of ball scheduled and this boy was the chief player. All the college was thrown into gloom because they saw defeat without this boy. But he came back directly from his father's funeral in time and said, "I am going to get into that game and do my part." He snatched victory from the very jaws of what seemed to be defeat; and when it was all over they gathered around him, when he was sobbing, and asked how he could play like that. He said to his comrades: "My blind father and I have been chums since mother died, and as he left me, he told me to go back and play the game just as I was scheduled, and said: 'Son, maybe I will see you.' And I think my father was seeing me and bidding me do my best."

But higher than such a witness as that is our glorious Lord, who watches on every part of the field; we must not do less than our best, until the day is done.

Once when the chaplain preached before the good and great Queen Victoria on the "Coming of Jesus," the Queen was moved that day as they had never seen her moved before. When he was through preaching they signaled him aside, and the chaplain asked: "Why have you been so moved today?" She said: "Because the Lord of lords is coming and I wish I could be here when Jesus comes, so that I might take off my crown and lay it at His feet."

My fellow Baptists, are we ready today to go to the mercy seat, repenting of all our sins? Let me go to the mercy seat; perhaps I ought to be the first of all; are we ready to go to the mercy-seat to offer our very lives for the redemption of Texas and America and the world?

Then, at last, we will hear that word given us in the nineteenth chapter of Revelation: "And a voice came out of the throne, saying, Praise our God, all ye His servants, and ye that fear Him, both small and great. And I heard as it were the voice of a great multitude, and as the voice of many waters, and as the voice of mighty thunderings, saying, Alleluia! for the Lord God omnipotent reigneth. Let us be glad and rejoice, and give honour to Him: for the marriage of the Lamb is come, and His wife hath made herself ready."

(The above message was delivered as the Convention Sermon of the Baptist General Convention of Texas, in Waco, Texas, on November 23, 1916).

SERMON II

The Adequacy of Christ

SERMON II

The Adequacy of Christ

*For the Scripture saith, Whosoever
believeth on Him shall not be put
to shame.*   ROMANS 10:11

IN THIS first service of our spring revival, I desire
to speak upon the "Adequacy of Christ," as suggested by a
sentence in Paul's letter to the church at Rome. Paul's letters
and sermons were always Christ-centered. This sentence,
found in the eleventh verse of the tenth chapter of Romans,
discloses the central note of all evangelical preaching: "For
the Scripture saith, Whosoever believeth on Him shall not be
put to shame." The careful Bible reader will observe that I
have quoted from the Revised Version in this text which
brings out the truth more clearly. Whatever Paul's theme, he
always linked it up with Christ. To the Corinthians (I Cor.
2:2) he wrote: "I determined to know nothing among you
save Jesus Christ and Him crucified." To the Galatians (Gal.
6:14) he said: "God forbid that I should glory save in the
cross of the Lord Jesus Christ." And again to the Corinthians
(II Cor. 4:5) he said of himself: "We preach not ourselves,
but Christ Jesus the Lord; and ourselves your servants for
Jesus' sake."

Paul realized and unhesitatingly affirmed that there is only
one adequate hope and help for humanity, and that such hope
and help are to be found in Christ and in Him alone. Surely,
it is of infinite moment that we follow his example in this
great matter of giving our witness for Christ. He always
pointed people to Christ as the one and only adequate hope

and help for them, for the present and for the unfolding and never-ending future.

Just before Paul's declaration in our text, he laid bare his heart. He said: "I say the truth in Christ, I lie not, my conscience bearing me witness in the Holy Ghost, that I have great heaviness and continual sorrow in my heart. For I could wish that myself were accursed from Christ for my brethren, my kinsmen according to the flesh. My heart's desire and prayer to God for Israel is that they might be saved." First of all, and most of all, and before all else and through and after all else, Paul pointed the people ever to the Lamb of God who taketh away the sins of the world.

The mission—the main business—of every friend and follower of Christ is to give witness always so clearly and so urgently that men and women hearing that witness shall understand that there is just one way out for mankind, and that way is Christ. This matter of witnessing for Christ and winning people for Christ, of reminding everybody that salvation alone is by Christ, is not incidental or secondary, but it is a matter of vital and supreme moment for us all. It is a time for all of us in Dallas and in America and in the world who profess to be followers of Christ, in every way we can, wisely and faithfully to remind the people that they are hurrying through time and into eternity and that there is only one adequate hope and help for mankind—just one—and that one is Christ. Here is our mission. This must be our witness.

The care of souls is the primary and central and supreme and unceasing task of every Christian in the world, without any exception. The first word in Christ's marching orders to His people is: "Go and make disciples." The early Christians, in obedience to Christ's orders, witnessed and testified in such a fashion as to make a mighty imprint on the world of their day. Of them it was said that they "turned the world upside down" by the words of their witness and the testimony of their lives.

When Christ came, Roman law had failed; Greek philosophy had failed; Oriental mysticism had failed: all had failed. And all remedies, except the remedy which is in Christ, have failed in our day. We have tried big business; we have tried diplomacy; we have tried statecraft; we have tried war; we have tried secular education! And the Lord still asks: "Wherefore do you spend money for that which is not bread, and your labor for that which satisfieth not?" God said to us through Jeremiah: "My people have committed two evils; they have forsaken Me, the fountain of living waters, and hewed them out cisterns, broken cisterns that can hold no water." Let us leave off these insufficient and failing remedies offered by the world. For our present and eternal welfare, let us try Christ! We must follow Him, or perish!

This witness, this testimony, this example should be the master passion of every Christian in the world. You say, "It ought to be the master-passion of the preacher," and you are right. Woe betide the people if the preacher be not a true witness and a faithful shepherd of souls! Woe betide the people! "Oh son of man, I have set thee a watchman. And if thou failest to watch, and evil shall overtake the one over whom I have appointed thee to watch, then will I require his blood at thy hand." Oh, the responsibilities of a preacher! One's heart fairly shrinks with the thought of the responsibilities of a preacher!

Rutherford, a glorious preacher in Scotland generations ago, left a diary for our instruction—and gracious instruction it is! As you scan that diary, you can see Rutherford's tears and feel the heartbreak, as he makes his cry to God to enable him to help the people: "Oh, if these souls from Anwoth will meet me at God's right hand, my heaven will be two heavens in Emmanuel's land!" I would paraphrase it and say: "Oh, if these souls in Dallas will meet me at God's right hand, my heaven will be two heavens in Emmanuel's land!" Surely, the preacher must be a passionate seeker after the souls of men.

37

Who else is to care? Parents are to care. They cannot abdicate nor delegate their responsibilities. I do not see how any man can keep from having a shadow across his heart, darker and heavier than my words can say, when his family is going to ruin spiritually. One wonders how a father or mother can go on, with a child or children out of Christ. How can parents be worldly and careless while their children are on the downward way? They may be in their graves before three days are past. How can parents be careless?

Every time the Lord lays a little babe on the hearts of young parents, there goes with the child a commission: "Take this child and rear it for Me." That commission is from God, and if parents put other things first, and evil overtakes the child, one day with broken heart the father shall stand in the gate as did David of old and wail out the piercing, poignant cry: "Oh my son, Absalom, my son, my son, Absalom! Would God I had died for thee, O Absalom, my son, my son!" I have heard that cry in Dallas. How can parents be careless, be prayerless, be worldly, be indifferent, be inconsistent, with the child or children being molded and shaped by them for all time and eternity! How can parents be careless concerning the spiritual welfare of their children?

The home is God's first institution for mankind. I repeat what I have said scores of times in your hearing. I am more concerned about the American home than I am concerned about any one thing in American life. There is much in American life that gives me great concern now. There are drifts, there are signs, there are tokens, there are influences that entail peril for this country. But I am more concerned about the American home than I am concerned about any other one thing. There seems to be a conspiracy to destroy the old-fashioned, quiet, prayerful, God-honoring home. If we are not watchful, we shall lose our taste for reading—solid, substantial reading—because of the manifold features of entertainment and because of the endless bid of the radio for our time and attention.

The primary business of parents is to train up their children in the nurture and admonition of the Lord. Parents have no place for smiles over their boasted achievements, though they may pile up bank deposits and have vast treasures of material wealth, if their children are on the road to destruction, giving no evidence of interest in the supreme things of God.

Yes, parents are to care for the spiritual welfare of their children. I adjure you to give your best attention to the highest welfare of those precious children committed to your care. The supreme responsibility is yours. You parents should and can do more to mold those young lives than anyone else in the world. Mold them, shape them, train them, while they are young by your godly precept and example, and when they are old they will not likely depart therefrom.

Teachers are to care. The teacher sits on a throne. He may have only six little ragged boys, but he is on a throne. The teacher who does not understand that his opportunities with these children, and his responsibilities for them, are enough to make the archangels tremble — the teacher who does not understand that should forsake his teacher's calling and go elsewhere, to be a blacksmith or something else and not to trifle with the young life of our children. Teachers are to care. Melanchthon, the scholar and philosopher of the Reformation, rightfully said: "To train one youth is a greater achievement than the military conquest of Troy." Teachers are to care—and, in particular, Sunday School teachers. The Sunday School teacher who does not have a burden for the class, for each and every member of the class and who does not say: "My heart's desire and prayer to God is that every member of my class might be saved" — the Sunday school teacher who does not have that kind of burden for the class should do one of two things. He should give up the class, saying, "I will not face it," or, which is far better, he should repent and do his best to bring each member of that class to the Son of God. Sunday School teachers are to care!

Who else is to care? Every Christian is to care. All Christians are to care. The humblest Christian under the sound of my voice can point souls to Christ. Every Christian has as much as one talent. Most of us have just one. Every Christian can point people to Christ. The needle woman can; the wash woman can; the humble clerk can; the groceryman can; the cab-man can; every Christian can point people to Christ. And that is our business—primary, central, supreme, and unceasing—that is our business.

I have told this congregation about two men, one in the North and one in the South, but their stories will do to tell again. The one in the South was a great banker. He told me the story himself and some of his men told me more, which was very much in his favor. He said he became much concerned about the employees in his bank, which was one of the big banks of the South. He had such concern about them that one day he called them all together for an evening meal and with fear and trembling they came. They said: "Maybe this is our final contact with him; he is going to get rid of us; he is going to change things." When the dinner was over, he arose and said: "I have called you together first of all because I want to tell you how much I appreciate you and then I hurry to tell you that I want to ask you to forgive me, if you can, for I have been a Christian for years and years, and I have never talked to any one of you personnally about your soul. The Christian can do better than that. I could have done better; I ought to have done better. You probably have the impression that I think bank deposits are more important than the souls of the people. I really do not think that, but I have acted as though I did. I want you to forgive me, if you can." And then he poured out his heart to that group, the majority of whom were already Christians, and said so through tears and lifted hands. But a little group of them lifted their hands indicating that they were not Christians and the bank president turned preacher and exhorted them and before a week had gone by, he had won them all to Christ. That was a great scene in a Southern city.

But in a Northern city, a certain Presbyterian pastor's heart was greatly discouraged. Months had gone by and not a soul had been converted, not one, and he was greatly discouraged. He called his elders together, and said to them: "I am thinking about resigning. People are not being converted and a church is to win people to Christ. I am wondering if I ought to resign as pastor of the church."

Then the elders said: "Oh, no, your preaching is very edifying." And he said: "Edifying for what? You elders come on Sunday morning, and heaven alone knows where you are Sunday night. One in a dozen of you come to prayer-meeting; heaven alone knows where the others are on prayer-meeting night. Edifying for what? A church is to win people for Christ and the members are to fortify and undergird the services. They are to be 'living epistles' walking up and down the street, glorifying God in a manner that even the devil must respect." Then, with deep feeling, he said: "Things will have to change or I am going to resign as your pastor. And that is not all. I think you elders ought to resign also. I think a new crew ought to be in charge at this church. Every one of you, I think, should give up your work as I certainly shall, if things do not improve." Then he asked the senior elder: "Did you ever win a soul to Christ in your life?" And he said, "Never." Then he asked this same question of each elder and not one of them could say, "Yes, I have won a soul to Christ."

That talk marked an epoch in the lives of all that company, preacher and elder alike. That great senior elder went to his business house the next morning and said to his right-hand man: "Bob, let me see you alone." And when they were alone he said: "Bob, have I not been a good friend to you, a kindly friend?" Bob said: "You certainly have. Anybody in the world is to be congratulated who has you for his friend." Then the elder said: "No, I have not been a good friend.

I have been a church member from my young manhood, and I have known you for years and years; we have talked day in and day out through those years and I have never said a word to you about the main thing. I have been quite remiss in my treatment of you. We are both at eternity's door and I claim to be the friend of Christ, put here to help lead men to Him, and I have never said one word to you about Christ in all these years." He sobbed out his confession to Bob, his chief ally in business. With the doors shut, he said: "If you do not mind, we will kneel down and I will try to pray." And he prayed, mostly for himself, then he prayed a few words for Bob, and when the prayer was finished, Bob arose and said: "I yield to Christ; right now I yield to Him."

The story goes that this big business man won every man in his employ to Christ, and that the other elders through the week won thirty men who offered themselves for membership in the church the following Sunday, saying: "We have found the Saviour and these elders pointed us to Him."

I think I could lie down and die in peace if my men would live and witness like that. I would say like Simeon of old, "Now, Lord, let thy servant depart in peace for I have seen Thy salvation."

Every Christian is to care. And furthermore, every Christian is under solemn obligation to bear his or her witness concerning Christ and His power to save. The world needs to have that witness borne. Right here in Dallas there are many thousands of men and women, boys and girls, who are groping in darkness, who know not Christ. They are lost and undone. Is it not true that we Christians are guilty before God if we withhold from them the witness that we can and ought to bear? My dear deacons, and teachers, and members —hundreds of you, yes, thousands of you—is not your duty and glorious privilege of witnessing for Christ to the lost people all around you both clear and urgent? In these days of desperate need and blessed opportunity will you not go afield among the people, as did the early Christians, humbly, prayerfully, faithfully, lovingly bearing your witness and giving your testimony as to your Saviour, who is able to save unto the uttermost all who will accept Him and trust Him? You can do that, and you will do that if you really care about the salvation of the lost and if you have a great love for Christ who died for them and for you.

Paul points the way for us. He uses God's Word: "For the scripture saith, Whosoever believeth on Him (on Christ), shall not be put to shame." That is Paul's method. He appeals to the Scriptures, and that is his appeal. *"The scripture says . . ."*; not *"The church says . . . ."* Our source of authority is the Holy Scriptures. All our creeds and conduct and opinions are to be tried by the Word of God, not by anything else. "The Scripture saith!" Paul's appeal was to the Scriptures. He followed Jesus when he preached. Jesus appealed to the Scriptures. In His very first sermon, Jesus quoted from Isaiah. And in His great wilderness temptation with Satan, He appealed to the Scriptures. He hurled the Scriptures into the face of Satan and repelled him.

All the apostles, following the example of Jesus and Paul, said: "As saith the Scriptures." And Paul points us to the source of all our help: "The scripture saith, Whosoever believeth on Christ shall not be put to shame." You will never be confounded—you will never be put to shame—if you will put your case in the hands of Christ. If you will believe on Him, rest on Him, lean on Him, commit your way to Him, the Scriptures say you will never be put to shame. Christ meets the test. He meets the test of life. Oh, what a test it is! I can take you in twenty minutes from this place to men and women who have lost their businesses but they are not bitter at all. They say: "We have Christ left." I can take you in a few minutes to people whose dearest earthly treasures are gone, but they are singing through their tears: "Don't you know He cares?" They are singing that now. Christ meets the test of life.

And then He meets the test of death. I have been called three or four times during the week just gone and, in every case at the funeral, the evidence was overwhelming that the departed one met that test when the test came, the test of death. John Wesley, great old hero of the faith, said: "Our people die well." Some of us, in our smaller sphere, can say like Wesley, "Our people die well."

Yesterday I buried one whom, years and years ago, I buried with Christ in beautiful baptism. He had been ill for a while. He sent me word: "I am ready; my time is at hand; I am ready to go and am unafraid. Back yonder, you pointed me to Christ, the source of all comfort and life and salvation and I go now, unafraid to meet Him." Our people die well.

Christ meets the test of eternity. He meets the test of what is beyond. You remember that terrible tragedy which occurred in East Texas two or three years ago, when about three hundred school children were burned to death in one of the most heart-breaking tragedies of modern times. The horrors of it still chill us beyond words. There was a little boy, a tiny little fellow five years of age, whose little sister was burned to death in that awful holocaust. The little boy of five said to his little friend: "Do you know where my sister is?" His little friend said: "She is in the grave." "No," he said, "she is not in the grave; she is in heaven with Jesus and she is having the best time you ever heard of in your life." The little fellow had it right: "At home with the Lord." Christ never fails. He meets the test of eternity and all the other tests.

Oh, are not we Christians ready afresh to give Him the best that is within us? Is not the lukewarm Christian resolved to say: "I will put away my lukewarmness. I will repent of my backsliding. I will go in the way marked out by Christ for His friends."

The last thing David Livingstone wrote in his diary was: "Jesus, my Saviour, my King, my God, I re-dedicate my all to Thee to be and to do for Thee the best that I can until the day is done." Can you not do the same thing, and do it today? Are there not men and women listening to me who, down in their hearts, have made the surrender to Christ but have held back their confession of it? Are you not ready to come out of all hesitation and inaction and disobedience, and follow Christ for your sake and for the sake of others bound up with you, and for the sake of Christ who died for us all? Are you not ready to come out of your secret discipleship and say: "Yes, I lean on Christ: I have put my case in His hands once and for all, and I mean by His help to live for Him"? Are you not ready to take your place in the church with His people?

And is there not the man or woman here ready to say: "I am ready today to begin. I am ready today to yield; ready today to decide; ready today to surrender; ready today to start with Christ. Dear Lord, I put my case in Thy hands; I give Thee myself; I accept Thee as my Saviour in Thine own great sovereign way; I surrender to Thee and I make my decision that Thou mayest be my Savior from today"? Are you now ready to make that decision?

> "Oh happy day that fixed my choice
> On Thee, my Saviour and my God."

Who says: "Today I am ready to follow Him"?

As this great audience of Christian people, who care and pray and love, sing an old-fashioned song, who of you will come saying: "I am a church member elsewhere but I desire to unite with this church by letter of transfer"? Or, "I am making my public confession of Christ; I have not been His follower but I start today; I decide today: I yield to Christ as my Saviour today." Who comes as we sing our hymn?

> "Oh happy day that fixed my choice
> On Thee, my Saviour and my God.
> Well may this glowing heart rejoice
> And tell its raptures all abroad."

SERMON III

Why Christ Died

S E R M O N   I I I

Why Christ Died

~~~~~~

Christ died for us.
ROMANS 5:8

FROM day to day as the people have gathered in this hall and now again this Thursday noon, the desire has been and is in my heart, deeper than I can say, so to speak that I may enhearten and help the people and especially those who are not on the side of and in the service of Christ. Not to be esteemed as eloquent or clever would I speak to you or to anyone else but, rather, would I speak ever to point my sinning, sorrowing, suffering fellow humanity to Him who died for us, to Him who is the one and only adequate helper for us in time and in eternity.

The question of questions is: How may a life stained by sin be made right with the perfect and holy God? Every one of us must give his personal account to God. How may we give that account in safety and in peace?

The question for our meditation today calls us back to that central and supreme question. It is a question which Christ Himself asked two of His perplexed disciples as they journeyed along the Emmaus road, to whom Christ joined Himself after His resurrection. They were greatly perplexed and cast down. They had misunderstood the great purpose of Christ's coming. They had thought He would reign in temporal, triumphant power but He was dead and in His grave. The crucifixion took place three days before and all sorts of rumors were afloat concerning Him whom they laid in Joseph's new tomb. As He journeyed with those perplexed men, He commenced talking to them and presently brought

49

them to this central question: "Ought not Christ to have suffered these things?"

This question calls us back to the foundation of Christ's own divine gospel of salvation. And this question has bound up with it two central truths for our meditation this hour. First, the awful fact of sin and, second, God's divinely provided remedy for sin. These two facts are hard by each other all through the Holy Word of God.

First, let us think of the solemn, awful fact of sin and that sin must be suffered for. Men would have to grant that fact if they did not believe the Bible at all and men do grant it everywhere, even where the light of the Bible has not reached. Laws to a remarkable degree take cognizance of that fact. Individual governments to a greater or lesser degree fashion their statutes around the principle that sin is something that requires punishment. The moral conscience of the world would be shocked by the teaching that sin was not to be punished. Civilization itself would be imperiled if we withheld from sin the punishment it calls for. Not even sentiment should pervert our sense of justice and righteousness. God has put elements within our nature which rise up with this insistence often and most painfully, that sin must be punished.

Memory—what haunting power there is in one's memory! It has the strange faculty of turning back the hands of the clock in one's' life and reaching up into the secret cabinets and unlocking them and bringing things out which one would like never to think of again. Those dark hours which are lived over through memory remind us that sin must be punished. God has given us memory and its haunting power is something unspeakably pathetic. He has given us the power of conscience and how poignant that power is at certain times in one's life. The power of conscience tells us that sin must be punished. Conscience may seem to sleep for a season and may seem to be dull and dead and unresponsive; but in the crucial hour, in the moral crises, conscience will make its cry felt and heard, even after the most solemn and painful fashion.

History, both sacred and secular, gives formal attestation to that fact. Take the pages of Bible history—what awful chapters stand out like spectres in the night through the awful power of conscience! In the case of Judas —who sold Jesus for thirty pieces of silver (about fifteen dollars in our money) —after a few hours, goaded as he was fairly to desperation by conscience, he came back to the Chief Priests, with whom the trade was made, the ill-fated bargain, and threw down the thirty pieces of silver with the cry: "Let's turn back, let's undo what we have done. I have betrayed innocent blood! Take the money back — it hounds my conscience and my brain! Take it back!" And they laughed him to scorn and, goaded by conscience, he went out and took his own life. Conscience has that awful power in human life!

John the Baptist was put in prison by Herod because he dared to denounce the king for improperly consorting with Herodias, his brother Philip's wife, who was by his side. John stood before Herod and said, "It is not lawful for thee to have her," and explained that there would be a day of reckoning with a righteous God. The woman bitterly resented the rebuke of the plain preacher. She bided her time, and the day came when her daughter danced before Herod and so pleased him that he asked what she would like for him to give her. She had been prompted by her mother; so she said, "I would like the head of John the Baptist, the man who rebuked you and my mother." Think of a girl making a demand like that! Herod winced under that demand, for he feared the people. But sodden and seething in sin as he was, he commanded the executioner to carry out this awful request and soon he brought the head of this fearless preacher for the dancing girl to carry to her mother. The horrible deed was done. The man who rebuked Herod and Herodias publicly could rebuke them no more.

Weeks and months passed, and the fame of Jesus spread abroad. His deeds and his works were attracting the people throughout all Galilee. When Herod heard of the wonderful works of Jesus, he said, "It is John the Baptist, risen from the dead." Oh, the cry of conscience! The cry of conscience!

Macbeth, one of the world's great dramas, lives because in it the vitality of conscience is recognized. Lady Macbeth, whose hands were stained with murder, revealed in her sleep-walking the state of her mind, as she would seem to wash her hands and say, "Will these hands ne'er be clean? Here's the smell of blood still. All the perfume of Arabia will not sweeten this little hand." It is the cry of conscience.

George Eliot, that keen-minded woman, marvelous in her portrayal of human life, gives in one of her books an account of a young girl who went to shame and ruin—earth's saddest sight is that! Every chivalrous man ought to set himself with all diligence and true manhood to obliterate from the earth every influence that makes for the down-dragging and damning of woman. The story said the girl went to ruin and, to hide her shame, put to death her little child—put it to death and hid it in the hedge. But a little later she was apprehended and brought to justice and judgment. And the kindly women all got around her—as they ought to have done—and pitied her and compassionated her and mothered her and tried to woo her away from dwelling on the horrible sin that had found its cumulation and culmination in her life. When they would pause for a moment, the girl would break forth with her pitiful refrain, "I hear—yes, I hear—I hear all that you have said, but will I always hear the cry of that little child that I put to death in the hedge? Will I always hear it?" That was the cry of conscience—the cry of conscience!

Conscience makes its cry that sin must be punished. There is an end of moral government if this be not so. What conscience cries and memory attests, the Holy Word of God which is the divine revelation of the mind of God and the will of God, the Holy Word of God comes with its clear statement that we all alike, in God's great moral government, are sinners. There is no difference. "All we like sheep have gone astray; we have turned every one to his own way." There is no difference. "We have all sinned and come short of the glory of God." "There is not a just man upon the earth, that doeth good and sinneth not." "Except ye repent, ye shall all likewise perish." That is the Word of God that came from the lips of the gentle Saviour. "Marvel not that I say unto you, Ye must be born again or ye can never see the kingdom of God."

All have sinned. Every human being is under the blight and infused with the poison of a moral sickness the name of which is sin. Is there any remedy? Is there any door of hope in the valley of Achor? Is there any balm in Gilead? Is there any physician that can heal this awful moral sickness which afflicts every human being? Thank God, there is! And here it is stated for us in four little Bible words: "Christ died for us." There is the hope for beaten, sinning, suffering, humanity! Christ died for our sins! Those little words state the central fact of the gospel of divine forgiveness and salvation. Before Christ died on Calvary, every smoking altar on which lay a bird or a beast, in sacrifice, pointed to the coming of that great sacrifice when Christ once and for all put away sin by the sacrifice of Himself. What is the secret of the power of the death of Christ to put sins away? "Christ died for us." "God commendeth His love toward us, in that while we were yet sinners, Christ died for us!" The Son of God loved you and me and gave Himself for us! "Substitution," you say, "is a great mystery." It is, and the principle of substitution is the greatest principle in all life.

Christ died for us.

> Jesus paid it all,
>   All to Him I owe—
> Sin had left a crimson stain;
>   He washed it white as snow.

That is the deepest note in human life—that Christ, the divine Redeemer, was a vicarious sufferer for sinners!

God might have dealt with sinners in one of three ways. He might have meted out absolute justice and compensation, and, if so, we would all have been destroyed. "If Thou, Lord, shouldest mark iniquity, oh, Lord, who shall stand?" Or God might have meted out absolute mercy. If that had been His plan it would have immediately put an end to moral government. But God is infinite in righteousness and mercy; He metes out to us absolute righteousness and absolute mercy, both in one. "Mercy and Truth are met together; Righteousness and Peace have kissed each other," in Christ. In His death absolute righteousness and absolute mercy were provided for the sinner at the same time. Why is Christ, alone, able to conquer our sins? Because God, the Eternal Father, whose law we all have broken, appointed Him for that divine purpose. Thus was established vicarious redemption for us because Christ, the divine Son, was spotless and sinless and could make that sacrifice; for Christ, in His own personality, is both God and man, as really God as though He were not man, as really man as though He were not God—the God-man in one personality. And He is able to be the one Mediator to win sinners back to God.

Oh, will you think of Him, dying for you, as this day you go your ways? After He died for you, what if you reject Him? What if you refuse Him? What if you will not have Him? Oh, will you think now, today—visualize it all—how they took Him and laid aside His robe and scourged Him and carried Him up the hill, the Christ, and nailed Him to the cross, and there 'twixt heaven and earth He died—the Friend of sinners died! It was for you! There is not any way out for you and me, except through the sacrifice of Christ.

No wonder the great old John Newton sang:

> In evil long long I took delight,
>   Unawed by shame or fear,
> Till a new object struck my sight
>   That stopped my wild career!

I saw One hanging on a tree
  In agony and blood!
He fixed His languid eye on me
  As near that cross I stood!

Oh, never to my latest breath
  Can I forget that look—
It seemed to charge me with His death
  Though not a word He spoke.

My conscience felt and owned my guilt
  And drove me to despair.
I knew my sins His blood had spilt
  And helped to nail Him there.

A second look He gave, which said:
  "I freely all forgive!
This blood is for thy ransom paid.
  I died that thou mightest live!"

"That thou mightest live!" What if you refuse Him? God forbid! God forbid, my dear, dear friends, that one in this room shall refuse to believe in Christ, your atoning Redeemer from sin!

SERMON IV

A Religion That Is Divine.

S E R M O N   I V

A Religion That Is Divine

Christ the power of God.
I CORINTHIANS 1:24

A RELIGION without a divine Saviour is a re-
ligion incompetent and insufficient for a needy, sinning, suffering, dying humanity. No man has moral sources within
himself sufficient to live the life that he ought to live. Systems
of ethics and of morals, however beautiful and worthy, will
not, and can not, transform men and women who have the
sense of sin in their lives—the sense of moral loss and lapse
and failure.

A while ago it was my privilege to speak some ten days to
the students of one of the country's largest universities. One
day I was waited upon by a group of Japanese students, who
desired an interview concerning the relative claims of their
country's religion and of our religion. I shall never forget
the interview. These Japanese were upper-classmen in the
university. They ranged themselves, some thirty men, in a
semi-circle about me, and then they began their questions.
How bright, how sharp, how searching, were their questions!
And presently they reached the question that they came to
ask. They said: "We follow Buddha, and you follow Christ.
Wherein does Christ excel Buddh? Buddha teaches this and
that," they said, "and Christ teaches this and that. Wherein
do the teachings of Christ excel the teachings of Buddha?"
Now, you can see that the issue was sharply joined. You

---

*Reprinted by permission of the Sunday School Board of the
Southern Baptist Convention. from *A Quest for Souls.*

know what I said, I take it. I said: "My fellow-men, Buddha does teach so and so, and standards that he sets up in many cases are beautiful. Christ teaches so and so. But Christ does more. Christ proposes to put a power divine into the life that will yield itself to Him. For illustration: Here are two trains of cars, and at the head of each is an engine. Christ puts His power into that Christian engine, so that it can pull any train of cars, no matter how weighty. Buddha does not talk about putting power into human life. Buddha does not talk about a strength superhuman and unrivaled and divine, which he will put into his followers. He simply holds up a standard out there. Christ holds up a standard and says: 'Come to Me, with all your weakness and ignorance and sin; let Me save and guide you, and I will help you in your life to realize that standard.' Christianity is the religion of a person, and that person is Christ; and Christ not only points us the way wherein we ought to walk, but He comes to us in our moral weakness and lapse and failure, and says to us: 'If you will honestly commit yourself to Me, that I may guide and master you, I will help you to live the life you ought to live.' And, therefore, Christianity outdistances all systems of human religion, by as much as God outdistances a man." It was good to see the response made by the students from afar to such appeal. .

Five little words this morning make our text: "Christ the power of God." They are found in the first chapter of Paul's first letter to the Corinthians.

Let me come at once to the heart of what I wish to say, by asking the question: How is Christ the power of God? I answer, first of all, He is the power of God in His own person. Christianity stands or falls with the person of Christ. What Hougoumont was to Waterloo, Christ's person is to Christianity. There have beeen only three views about the person of Christ—one that He was bad, another that He was mad, and the other that He was what He everywhere represented Himself to be; namely, that He was God come in the flesh. When

He was here there were those who affirmed that He was bad. They affirmed that He was in league with Beelzebub, the prince of demons. They said: "He hath an evil spirit, and is not to be trusted." And then there were those who affirmed that He was mad. They said: "He is beside himself." They said: "He is crazy." And then there stands out the third estimate of Him — that He was not bad, and that He was not mad, but that He was and is what He everywhere represented Himself to be—God come in the flesh.

When Jesus became a man, He said in effect to men, wherever He went: "I am God manifest in the flesh. I am God uncovered; I am God foreshortened, so that a man with all his limitations by reason of ignorance and weakness and sin can find God." The cry of the race through the ages has been: "Show us the Father, and it sufficeth us." Jesus came among men and everywhere represented Himself as the possessor of the attributes and the perfections of deity. That Jesus was and is in His own person the power of God is attested by what He said, and by what He did, and by what He was and is. I am compelled intellectually to believe that Christ was more than any mere man, no matter from what angle I look at Him.

Will you look at His words? They attest His deity, "Never man spake like this man." I do not wonder that when Daniel Webster had finished the reading of the Sermon on the Mount, he rose up with pale face and trembling voice, and said: "More than any mere man has spoken these words." Never man spake like this man. Christ's teachings concerning the great matters that pertain to life and conduct and man and sin and character and destiny are utterly revolutionary and transforming.

I am also compelled to believe that Jesus is more than any mere man when I look at His works. One of His appeals to men is: "Believe me, that I am in the Father, and the Father in me; or else believe me for the works' sake." From the cradle to the grave there was in the life of Jesus the outflashings of

His divine nature and power. When a little child yonder on His mother's heart, the shepherds came to worship Him and the Magi came with their rich gifts to lay before Him. When He was a child of a dozen years, yonder He was in the temple, and the questions that He both asked and answered broke to pieces the superlative wisdom of those learned doctors and teachers assembled in that temple. And when He began His public ministry, the winds and the waves obeyed Him, and sicknesses obeyed Him, and demons obeyed Him, and death obeyed Him. Jean Paul Richter was right when he said that Jesus with His pierced hand had lifted empires off their hinges, and had turned the stream of centuries backwards in its channel. And Lecky, the astute philosopher, was right when he said that the three short years of Jesus' public ministry had done more to soften and regenerate mankind than all the disquisitions of all the philosophers, and all the exhortations of all the moralists since the world began.

I am compelled to believe in Christ—that His own nature was divine and that in Him was the infinite power of God—when I look at His character. The standing challenge of Jesus to mankind is: "Which of you convicteth me of sin?" And the universal response to that challenge is stated in the language of Pilate: "I find no fault in Him." Horace Bushnell was right when he said that the character of Jesus forbids all possible classification of Him with any and all other men.

Behold Jesus, this Friday morning, not *a* Son of man, but *the* Son of man; for all humanity was summed up in Him. In all other men, goodness is but fragmentary and pitifully imperfect. In the character of Jesus, goodness is perfect and complete, wanting nothing. If you would look for the highest example of meekness, you would not look to Moses, but to Jesus, who was unapproachably meek and lowly in heart. If you would look for the highest example of patience, you would not look to Job, but to Jesus who, when He was reviled, reviled not again. If you would look for the highest example of wisdom, you would not look to Solomon, but to

Jesus, who spake as never man spake. If you would look for the highest example of zeal, you would not look to Paul, but to Jesus, about whom it has been written: "The zeal of thine house hath eaten me up." If you would look for the highest example of love, you would not look to John, who leaned on Jesus' bosom, but you would look to Jesus who, while we were yet sinners, so loved us as to die for us. Goodness in men, however wise and pure their character, is fragmentary and imperfect and incomplete. Goodness and perfection stand out in their entirety in the person of Jesus. Men sometimes say to me that they cannot believe in miracles, and in every case I ask them: "What will you do with Jesus of Nazareth? He is the miracle of the ages. Jesus of Nazareth—what will you do with Him? He is the outstanding miracle of all the centuries. What will you do with Jesus?"

> Forever God, forever man,
> My Jesus shall endure,
> And fixed on Him my hope remains
> Eternally secure.

It was said of Mozart that he brought angels down, and of Beethoven that he lifted mortals up. Jesus of Nazareth does both, and more. Jesus is God's way to man. Jesus is man's way to God. Jesus is the only true Jacob's ladder, by which a sinning man or woman, if he or she will leave sin behind, may mount up to be with God and to be like Him forever. Yes, Christ is the power of God in His own person. I marvel that intellectually every man in the world is not compelled to bow down before the person of Christ.

Nor is that all. Christ is the power of God in history. The standing marvel of the ages is Christ himself, the Rock of Ages. An humble prophet of Nazareth has gone up and down the earth, and has more influence, more sway, than all the teachers that earth ever saw combined.

Hushed be the noise and the strife of the schools,
 Volume and pamphlet, sermon and speech,
The lips of the wise and the prattle of fools,
 Let the Son of Man teach.

Who has the key to the future but He?
 Who can unravel the knots of the skein?
We have groaned and have travailed and sought to be free.
 We have travailed in vain.

Bewildered, dejected and prone to despair,
 To Him, as at first, do we turn and beseech.
Our ears are all open, give heed to our prayer.
 O Son of man, teach!

He is the incomparable teacher of all the ages, and beside Him earth's greatest teachers are as a flickering candle beside a great sun. Christ is the miracle of the centuries, and the church is His monument. The most glorious institution in all the earth is Christ's monument—His church. It is the fairest among ten thousand, and an institution supremely lovely and worthy. And Christ's gospel is the supreme instrument of human civilization. There is not and can not be any lasting civilization which excludes the teaching of Christ. You may have your systems of government, no matter how compact and militaristic and colossal; you may have your schemes of education, no matter how subtle and clever and adroit and scientific; but all systems human are doomed ultimately to go into the ditch, if the standards and teachings of Christ are flouted and disregarded. The World War is the demonstration of what I am saying on the most colossal scale in all human history.

And now I am coming to say the most important word of all to you, my brother men, my gentle sisters. Christ is the power of God in human experience. That is the vital word of all. Christianity employs always the scientific method of demonstration, that is, the method by experiment. Somebody once asked Mr. Coleridge if a man could prove the truth of Christianity, and Mr. Coleridge made the simple but complete reply: "Why, certainly. Let him try it." Christ comes to mankind and confidently says: "Come and see. Come and try me. Come and test me. Put me to the extremest test. Come and test me and see for yourself, if I do not give you to know that I am the power of God in human life. Come and test me, and you will sing thereafter, when your fellows ask you what has happened: 'Whereas I was blind, now I see.' Come and try me."

I am thinking now of a young woman, unusually trained and cultured, bedarkened in her spiritual nature by the direst kind of skepticism. She sought interview after interview with the preacher, and one day she said to him: "Sir, intellectually, I just cannot accept your preaching that Christ rose from the dead on the third day, as your Scriptures allege." Presently, the preacher said to her: "Well, what do you think about Christ—waiving for a moment the fact of His resurrection — what do you think of Him?" She said: "He is the fairest among ten thousand. He is the one altogether lovely. I cannot find any fault with Him. Everything about His words and about His works and about His character to the last degree appeals to me." Then the minister went on to say: "If He be the Son of God Himself, the power of God in His own personality, if that be so, do you wish to know it?" After a moment's pause, she said: "Assuredly, I do." Then the minister said: "You go alone and tell Him that you are vexed by doubt and held back by questions, but that you wish light, and that you will yield yourself to Him, who already has won your admiring appreciation; that you will yield yourself to Him, that He may teach you and help you and lead you in any way that He would have you go—just honestly yield yourself to Him. Try Him in that experimental way." She came back the next day with her face radiant like the morning, and said to the preacher: "I cannot prove by outside proof, that Jesus rose from the dead, but my heart knows He is alive, for He has made me alive."

He is to be experimentally tested, my fellow-men. He is to be tested. Let me tell you, I see enough in one week, as do these honored brother ministers of mine about me, to shut us up to the conviction that Christ is the power of God. We see enough in one week in our dealings with men to be shut up to that unhesitating conviction. To illustrate: One day there came to me the news that one of my fellow-workers had gone down in the awful maelstrom of business failure. Fine fellow, rising, battling nobly, but the tides had turned, and down he went, and I went out to his home with my heart in my throat, dreading to see him and his wife. As he met me at the door, he looked years older, but there was no trace of bitterness on his face or in his eye. He said, "We are glad to see you. You have heard about it?" I said, "Yes, I have heard, and I have come to kneel beside you, and together we will talk to Him who is able to turn the very shadow of death into morning. No man is to despair or to worry or to mope because all his property is swept away in a brief day." He said, speaking quickly: "Oh, no; we are not bitter about it at all. We did not sleep any last night. We got up several times in the night, and like two little children we knelt beside our bed, and we promised new devotion to the service of Christ. Oh, no, we have not a bitter thought at all." And from that day to this—and that was years ago—never have I heard a note of bitterness or reproach escape their lips, and time and again they have said to me: "But for Christ consciously in our hearts, we should have been submerged when that Black Friday came."

And then, on another day, I was summoned when one of our citizens lay a-dying, one of the most gifted scientists I have known, and also one of the noblest Christians. The sun sank to the west, and the sands of his life were galloping to the close, and I sat there by him, in response to his invitation that I come for a final conference, and he said various and sundry things to me, as I held his hand. I shall never forget one thing he said. It was this: "Oh, pastor, go on and preach Christ to men, and nothing else; for nothing else, sir, will suffice men who are in the grip of moral loss and failure and defeat. Men do not have moral resources within themselves to rise and climb. Sir, preach a divine Saviour to a lost world. Preach that only till the day of your death." That last conversation we had I can never forget. And then, when he quit talking like that to me, he said: "I should like to speak to the children," and the children were brought in, and he had his word, beautiful and blessed, for every child. And then, as his wife held that thin hand and bent over him and kissed the noble forehead, he said to her, with his whispers, as life's sands hastened to the end: "Mary, dear, you will know where to look for comfort and strength when I am gone." She said: "Indeed, I will." Then he said: "Mary, dear, four different times you and I have marched behind the hearse to the cemetery, to put away out there, under the flowers, one child, two children, three children, four children, and we came back, and every turn of the carriage wheels whispered to us that the grace of God was sufficient. Now, Mary, dear, when I shall go away, as I shall tonight, you will remember the Shepherd Psalm, and you will remember the fourteenth chapter of John, and you will remember always to call on Christ and be not afraid." And she kissed him, and said: "I will remember. I know whom I have believed, and am persuaded that He is able to keep that which I have committed unto Him against that day." And then he quietly began the recitation of that Twenty-third Psalm, and when he reached that heavenly sentence: "Yea, though I walk through the valley of the shadow of death, I will fear no evil, for thou art with me," he whispered, and we caught it: "See, Mary, He is with me now," and then he was gone to the yonderland. You should have seen her and the children bear their grief without any murmur. God's grace was sufficient for them, and all the people knew it.

And then, on still another morning, my phone rang and one of our young business men said to me: "Be ready. I will be at the door for you with a cab in a dozen minutes. I need you much just now." I was there at the door waiting when the cab drove up, and he jumped out of the cab, his face covered with tears and his agitation something pitiful, and I took his hand and said: "What on earth is it?" He said to me, with a plaintive sob, even with gasps of sobbing: "If you know how to pray, you must pray now, for our little girl is at death's door and the doctors give us no hope at all. Sir, if you know how to pray, you will ask God to spare her now." I said: "My friend, I will pray for her, but not the way you suggest. I would not pray the way you suggest even about my own little children. I will ask God, if it can comport with His will, to spare your little girl, but if that be not His will that He will fortify you and the mother, and give you grace and strength to face it all." And then he turned upon me wildly and said: "I suppose I could bear it if the little girl shall be taken, but the little girl's' mother is an invalid, and it will kill her if the little girl is taken." I said: "No, no, my friend; your wife is a joyful Christian. She has a secret you do not know anything about. She has a secret that will bear her up and fortify her in the cloudiest day that ever comes." By this time we had reached the home, and we went in. The gentle wife was beside the crib, stroking the little forehead with its flaxen curls about it, talking to the child as the sands of its life hurried to the close, and then talking to God. And as we stood by her, the young father looked at me with a gasp and said: "Isn't my baby dying right now?" I said: "Yes, my friend; she is dying right now." And then he left the room, unable to face the rest.

All too soon the little life was gone, and then after a few moments more the wife said to me: "Where is my husband?" I said: "I will find him, and I went out behind the cottage, and found him wild in his grief, and when he heard my footfall he turned to me and said: 'It is all over, isn't it?" I said: "It is all over." And then, with a wail never to be forgotten, he said: "You will see it will finish my poor little invalid wife." I said: "Not at all, my friend. She has a secret you do not know anything about. She has a power within her above the flesh, superhuman, God's own power. You come now and see." And we came on back, and at the door we paused, because she was kneeling by that baby again, and it seemed sacrilege to enter, as we heard her praying. She was thanking God for the little girl, even though she had only had her three or four years. She was telling the Master that she would always be a better woman, because He had given her the child. She was saying that it was "better to have loved and lost than never to have loved at all." And then she paused, and I said: "We will go in now, my friend." And as we entered, she came, the invalid that she was, toward us, and her face was radiant. There were tears upon it, but there were smiles deeper than the tears. She put her frail arms about the big shoulders of her husband, and said: "Poor, broken-hearted husband, mother is so sorry for you! Mother knows it is all right. Mother's heart is swept with peace. Little bits of heaven have come down, my husband, to me. Mother is so sorry for you." Then the big fellow turned to me with the cry: "If Jesus Christ can do that for my frail wife, let me kneel beside my dead baby, and you tell Christ for me that I will give up to Him right now." Of course, Christ saved him then and there.

Jesus Christ can do that. He does do it. Hundreds will so testify. He is the power of God in human life. Is He your power? God help you, if He is not! Oh, men, my brothers: oh, gentle women, my sisters, is Jesus Christ the power of your life? Is He your personal Saviour? Is He your Master, by your own glad assent and consent? Let Him be! I speak to you the sober truth this Friday morning, when I say you may go and drink from every spring on the face of the earth, and you may try the aroma of every flower that earth can give and you will come back desolate and dispirited and broken, without Christ. Earth cannot heal your malady. Earth cannot cure your hurt. Byron tried it—that brilliant, gifted Byron— and he penned this as the result:

69

My days are in the yellow leaf;
  The flowers and fruits of love are gone;
The worm, the canker, and the grief
  Are mine alone!

I read the confession the other day of one of the most prominent actresses today on the world's stage. Admirers found her after a brilliant performance—after her appearances had been often encored, and roars of applause had shaken the building—after it was all over, they found her sobbing like a broken-hearted child, and they said to her: "Why woman, you ought to be happy, unspeakably happy, even the happiest of women, because of such applause as your every appearance calls forth." But she answered: "Oh, my heart is broken. My heart longs for something better and surer than this." And it does, because God hath set eternity in the human heart; and the things temporal, therefore, cannot meet the cry of the eternal.

Oh, where shall rest be found,
  Rest for a weary soul?
'Twere vain the ocean's depths to sound,
  Or pierce to either pole.

Beyond this vale of tears
  There is a life above,
Unmeasured by the flight of years,
  And all that life is love.

There is a death whose pang
  Outlasts this fleeting breath.
Oh, what eternal horrors hang
  Around one's second death!

Lord God of truth and grace
  Teach us that death to shun,
Lest we be banished from God's face
  And evermore undone!

Are you willing for Christ to teach you? Are you willing for Him to be your Saviour? Are you willing for Christ to be your Saviour His way? He will never be otherwise. Are you willing for Him to be your Saviour His way, and that

He may master your life according to His will, which is infinite in wisdom and goodness? If you are, and will thus yield your life to Him, you shall know that Christ is the power of God in your own experience. Do you say, "Yes, today and now, I answer to Christ's call, yielding myself without reserve to Him that He may have His way with me from this hour forward forever"? How we rejoice with you in your destiny-determining decision, and we leave you with Him, who will never leave nor forsake the soul that trusts Him.

SERMON V

Think on These Things

S E R M O N   V

Think on These Things

~~~~~~

> *Finally, brethren, whatsoever things are true; whatsoever things are honest; whatsoever things are just; whatsoever things are pure; whatsoever things are lovely; whatsoever things are of good report, if there be any virtue, and if there be any praise, think on these things.*
> PHILIPPIANS 4:8

HOW much time and attention do we give to right thinking? The capacity to think lifts man above the physical world around him and separates him from the animal kingdom. But that capacity to think can be neglected and misused. The capacity to think is a great trust. As we think, so shall be our character. "As a man thinketh in his heart, so is he."

Paul gives wise counsel in our text. What is it? We are to think on the right things. We will agree that the control of our thoughts is an exceedingly difficult matter. It is purely personal. This is a realm in which the individual is master. No one can control the individual's thinking. Others may *influence* our thinking but they cannot *control* our thinking. The thought world is a realm in which the individual is absolute ruler.

We are restrained often from improper actions and from improper talk because of our surroundings, or because of business considerations, or self care, or other prudential reasons. These things restrain us often from behaving outwardly in an improper way, or from talking in an improper way.

But a very different situation obtains with reference to our thinking. We say that thought is free. To a remarkable degree it is. Our thoughts may be bad, and we can keep them to ourselves. We may think improper or low thoughts, thoughts little and mean, thoughts groveling and unworthy, and no one know anything about it. That very fact constitutes a great danger. Because the individual's thoughts can be kept secret, there is the peril that all the while that individual may be generating within himself or herself a vicious, corrupt, poisoned mentality. Therefore, we are summoned by God's Word to put a grip on our thoughts, to get our thoughts under discipline and see that they are directed to lofty and ennobling subjects.

The injunction of God's Word is to habituate yourself to think always on the right things and to put out of your thinking every wrong thing. One of the big battles of life is the battle to control our thoughts—our inner, silent, secret thinking, when nobody sees or knows but ourselves. We are summoned to set ourselves resolutely to think the right things and to refuse to think the wrong things. A destiny-determining battle of life is waged at this point. Here is the arena where the victory of life is won or lost.

This matter of individual thought control is so important that our happiness depends upon it. If we cannot learn to turn our thoughts to the right subjects and to meditate upon them and to refuse to think on wrong subjects, life shall be maimed and crippled and made miserably unhappy. Our very happiness is involved here. A man can, by training his mind on the right things, project himself into a high realm of happiness. If a man does not control his thinking and compel himself to turn from the wrong things, and to think on the right things, then he shall find himself groveling in the filth of a low plane of intellectual existence.

That is a very serious matter, the control of our thoughts; and our unconscious influence over other people is to a remarkable degree enwrapped in our thoughts. Our unconscious influence goes out over other people. The very thoughts that we think somehow get out, in ways multitudinous, and influence those around us.

That was a great word that Jesus said: "There is nothing hidden that shall not be revealed." Not simply in the judgment, by and by, but in the here and the now, there is nothing hidden that shall not be revealed.

I am thinking just now of a little child who shrank back from a handsome man. He was supposed to be upright and honorable and clean and moral and highminded and true, and yet he was nothing of the sort. He harbored low thoughts, base thoughts, selfish thoughts, bestial thoughts, debauching thoughts, undoing thoughts and the very harboring of them in himself, secretly wrought itself in the glance of his eye, the curl of his lips, in every lineament of his face, and when a tiny little girl of five or six summers came into his presence she shrank away from him.

Why is it that a good woman instinctively turns away from this or that character? It is the same powerful something within—the secret, silent, hidden thought which writes its power in every fiber and phase of one's moral and mental nature, and even in the physical nature also. The face is powerfully influenced by our thoughts. Full many a time a face is debauched and low, and you shrink when you look into that face. The thought within—not expressed, not published in the papers, not placarded on the sign-boards—the secret, ignoble thought has made its imprint on the human countenance.

Now the matter of what we shall think about is so vital that it must have our best attention. Why is that so? Because thought moulds character. "As a man thinketh in his heart, so is he." If he prefers to think groveling thoughts, muckraking thoughts, sensual thoughts, crooked thoughts, he is of that character.

Thought determines character. Therefore, we must give heed to our thought. If you entertain a bad thought, if you

77

hang there in your brain a foul thought, and pet it and coddle it and pamper it and keep it willingly it will do you hurt. One minute of it will leave you stained; you will be worse off because you cherished such visitor even for one minute.

Everything that we see about us was first a thought. This church building was first a thought in the architect's mind. The great inventions that come to be the wonder and surprise and marvel and convenience to mankind, each one was first a thought in the inventor's mind. Creation, wonderful creation, was first a thought in the mind of God. Sin that breaks out and shames and scars and burns was first a thought. Thought precedes sin. Now, therefore, thought is a matter of supreme moment, because thought molds character. "As a man thinketh in his heart, so is he."

I could not bring you then a more practical, a more vital, a more reconstructive, a more fundamental message than to summon you to think on the right things, to refuse absolutely to think on the wrong things. And the Bible here lists some of the right things on which we are to think. "Whatsoever things are honest, whatsoever things are just, whatsoever things are pure; whatsoever things are lovely, whatsoever things are of good report, think on these things." And the clear implication is that we are to decline consciously, habitually, and on high principle, to allow other thoughts— base, groveling, selfish, and sensual thoughts—to have a welcome at all in our hearts.

That means that just as in the Old World the gates to the cities had keepers to open or close them according to the applicant seeking admission, so must we have gate keepers standing at the door of our minds. And when a bad thought about anything or about anybody comes, saying, "Harbor me for a while, entertain me for a while, let me be your guest for a while," we are to refuse entrance to such visitor, and we are to say: "No such visitor can be admitted within the premises of my mind by my consent for one second." By a fixed, determined will, thoughts evil are to be excluded and thoughts good are to be welcomed and cultivated. Such decisions may not be easy but they are very vital to character.

There were three boys in a little country home far inland, away from the noisy world, and all three of them when they grew up made at once for the sea, and dedicated their lives to the sea—all three of them. Their mother was heart-broken. She could not understand it at all. She failed to see the point. She wanted them to live on the farm with her. But all three, when they reached their majority, left the farm for the sea. And they? The explanation was not hard to find. There was just one picture in that country home, and it was of a ship at sea, plowing the storm-tossed deep, beating its way in spite of wind and wave. It was the only picture in the house: the little boys thought about it and pondered about it until the sea and the storms and the tossing ship entered into their souls and, when they were grown, they all went to sea.

As we think in our hearts, so are we. Two girls occupied the same building. In one room there were pictures of noble women who had moved the world heavenward by their noble deeds. The girl who occupied this room looked on those pictures often and studied the faces of those good and great women morning, noon and night. In the same building there was another girl whose wall was hung with pictures, selfish, groveling, low pictures, suggestive of evil. The first girl, with her noble pictures, climbed the way of the highest; and the second girl, with the degrading and basely suggestive pictures upon her wall, went the way of doom and death. No one need have been surprised at the fate of the two girls, had they known about the pictures on the walls.

Now that is just as simple and inevitable as breathing. The food taken into the mind is either good or bad for the mental life, just as food taken into the body is either good or bad for the physical life. If it be bad food, the effect will be bad; if it be good food, the effect will be wholesome and healthful. The matter, then, of our thoughts—of our secret thoughts that are kept within—are of supreme moment. Evil thoughts that we harbor weaken and lower our moral natures; good thoughts, that we welcome and keep and hold and cherish and reinforce, make us stronger for every good thing in this world and in the world to come.

This matter is so important that we must do something about our thoughts. We must set ourselves resolutely, as I have indicated, to keep out of our minds bad thoughts of every kind. They, like weeds, will come voluntarily and unexpectedly. We cannot prevent them from coming, but we can prevent them from staying. We need not allow them lodgment for one moment. We can displace evil, ignoble and selfish thinking with good thinking. That requires effort, purpose, decision, habit and conscience. We are summoned, on high principle, to put all low and groveling and debauching and down-pulling and undoing thoughts from our minds. In their place we are to put in our minds good, high, pure, unselfish, lovely and noble thoughts, just as Paul urges us to do in our text. We must displace the evil with good. "Nature abhores a vacuum," and so does the human mind. Let the good thoughts drive out the bad thoughts!

If we do that, great shall be our triumph, beautiful shall be our character. Glorious shall be the life, if we wisely think on the right things and thereby exclude the wrong things from our thoughts.

What an important truth this is for young people! If they think on a bad thing, and brood over it, and turn it about in their minds, as the tinder within them is ready to be ignited, when the touch of the tempter comes at some critical moment, they are in danger of becoming corrupted, soiled and defiled because of the harboring of evil thoughts.

Now, if thoughts that are unclean and impure and unworthy get into the mind—thoughts that you would not be willing for your mother to know about—thrust yourself resolutely into the fight and put them out. But it is not enough to resist evil, it is not enough to overcome evil. In addition thereto, we must put good in its place.

Then, there is the question of the kind of literature to be read. We must avoid trashy literature—foul, gangrenous literature, low, tainted, and debauched literature, covered as it is with the superficial and the fantastic. We should put such literature as that in the fire, and in its place we should read wholesome, positive, vital and life-giving literature.

The mental and social atmosphere in which we live greatly influences our thinking. If it be unwholesome, foul and degrading, we should turn from it and seek the higher continually. If we are to control our thoughts, we need every possible reinforcement from within and from without. Environment is a powerful factor in fashioning character. It is vastly important that living conditions be wholesome and uplifting.

Your influence outward, your unconscious influence, is involved in this matter of your secret thought, for what is within you gets out. What is hidden shall be revealed. The way is made plain for us. We are to put in the place of the bad that which is good, and drive out the bad with the good.

A boy brought his mother's picture to the city. To some of us he said: "When the temptation is terrible, I can expel it by getting back to my room and looking at mother's picture, which I have hanging on the wall. I can look at it and all my foul thoughts and evil desires are utterly given up, in one moment, when I gaze on the face of my patient, glorious, Christian mother."

Let us pursue that thought a bit further. What do you think of Jesus? If you will think the right thoughts about Him; if you will think enough about Him to trust Him and have Him for your companion; if you will think enough to let Him regulate your life and control your ways, then victory increasingly shall be your portion. Jesus will help that one who, with deliberate intention and purpose, thinks on Him and trusts Him. He will give to that one the victory over every foe that assails.

There are three great words which gather about Jesus that explain the victory. First is the word *light*. Jesus gives light. How important light is! Evil has a way of flourishing in the dark. Man cannot think as well in the night as in the day. He cannot think as nobly in the darkness as in the light. When the morning comes and the birds are singing and the golden day is on, one's thoughts are happier and nobler and they are more beautiful than in the darkness. Jesus says: "Put your thoughts on me, because I am the light of the world. I will lead you out of the darkness, the superficial and the low will be given up if you think on me."

Then there is another word about Jesus, and that word is *love*. We think about what we love. We think much about whom we love. If a man does not think much and often about his mother, he does not love her. If he does not think much and often and with unspeakable tenderness about his wife and children, he does not love them. If we love Christ truly we shall think much about Him and those thoughts will be a transforming power within us. We well know that love for a good woman has often proved to be a powerfully reclaiming and redemptive influence in the life of a wayward son or husband. How much more can one's love for Christ be a transforming and regenerating force in that one's life. Love for Christ and thoughts about Him can be the most powerful expulsive force of all to help us have clean minds and pure hearts.

There is still another word about Jesus, and that is the word *life*. Jesus came to lift our poor, little strangled lives out of the mire and up into abundant life. And if you put your thoughts on Jesus and trust Him, He will redeem your life from its sordidness, from its baseness, and He will help you to think on the lofty things indicated in our text. The only safe and sane course is for you to accept Jesus for your Confidant, your Saviour and your Guide. If you keep close to Christ, your life shall be one of increasing mastery over the evil and the low, and His light and love shall enrich your life and crown it with blessed victories both in time and eternity.

Perhaps there is somebody here tonight who would like to accept and confess Jesus as Saviour and Lord—somebody who says: "I am insufficient for my task. I cannot control thought or desire. I cannot control life. I am beaten and tossed about and carried down. I am not rising. I am not climbing. I am drifting. I am sinking and from the depths I cry to the Saviour, who says: 'Him that cometh unto me, I will in no wise cast out'! I surrender to Him and I tell Him, 'Lord, save me or I perish.' I will trust Him whatever comes."

He will forgive you: He will put a great power in you, and then He will Himself companion with you until the day is done.

Is there somebody here tonight who says: "I do surrender to that Saviour"? Come while we sing:

> "Out of my bondage, sorrow and night,
>   Jesus, I come; Jesus, I come;
> Into Thy glorious freedom and light,
>   Jesus, I come to Thee."

SERMON VI

Permanent Profit

SERMON VI

Permanent Profit

~~~~~~~~~~~~~~~~~~~~~~~~~~~~~~~~~~~~~

> *But godliness is profitable unto all*
> *things, having promise of the life*
> *that now is, and of that which is*
> *to come.*   I TIMOTHY 4:8

ANYTHING which is profitable for the life that now is, and for that life which follows this and is never to end, certainly demands our best attention. "Godliness is profitable unto all things, having promise of the life that now is, and of that which is to come." Here are two lives mentioned, yet closely joined—the life that now is and the life which is to come, closely joined. Death, which is coming to us all, is but a slight break. What a man is at death, so shall he be beyond death. You would reverse every law of science and philosophy, if that were not so. Death is but the dark archway through which the river flows for just a moment. Every man shall go to his own place. Moral gravity is just as fixed and clear as is physical gravity. The most awful thought that ever went through my brain or yours is the thought of missing the highest and passing at death into a state fixed, unchanging, eternal. I have never had another thought so serious as that when I come to think of the human soul, of such outreaching capacities and possibilities, which misses it. As the tree falls so shall it lie. Jesus said to John on Patmos: "He that is unjust, let him be unjust still; and he that is holy, let him be holy still." And he was speaking of destiny.

The question confronts us: How may one make the most of this life and of yonder life, of time and of eternity, of this world and the world which is to come? That is the question suggested by the text. That is the big question confronting every human soul. That is the supreme question. How may one make the most and the best and the highest of this life and of that life? Death is but a slight break. Here you are in time, and then in one moment you are in eternity. You are there what you were here. If you are positionized wrongly here, when you come to the gates of the grave you will be positionized wrongly beyond. Destiny is determined this side the gates of the grave.

Now, how may one make the most of this life and that one, of time and of eternity, one a longer chapter than the other but inseparable? I must deal with eternity. I must deal with the next world. Issues and vitalities inescapable concern me, for the next world as well as for this. Now, the big question is, How to make the best and the most and the highest of both time and eternity, of this life and that which is to come? Our text tells us. If we are to make the most of this life—seventy years, maybe, sixty or forty, or more or less—if we are to make the most of this life, then godliness is to be exalted by us. We are to be for God. Reverentially we are to fear Him. Honestly we are to trust Him. Sincerely we are to serve Him, and in our lives we are to seek to incarnate His precepts and illustrate and make vital His teachings. "Godliness is profitable unto all things, having promise of the life that now is, and of that which is to come." It is of supreme importance for one to be for God in this life. It is profitable, supremely profitable, for this life.

Satan comes with all his arts and devices and confronts every human soul right at that point. Satan contests the doctrine that Christianity is worthwhile in this life. I suppose he does not contest it for the life to come. When the soul is considering the great claims of Christianity, I suppose that Satan does not assume or dare to question its worth for the life to come. His task ever is to get time, to get delay, to get procrastination—the thief of time, and likewise and sadly, the thief of souls. Satan's great task is to get a stay of decision, a delay of action. He said to me: "It is a good thing for you to be a Christian when you get to be an old man and life is uncertain and death is imminent, but now, in the morning of life, with the rainbows of hope spanning all the horizon, what would you do with Christianity now?" He said to me: "What would you do with Christianity in the great courts?" to which my ambitions and thoughts and plans and progress turned. "What would you do with Christ there? What would you do with Christ out on the hustings? What would you do with Christ in the forum? What would you do with Christ in the practical, busy, matter-of-fact world? Satan dared to say to me—I take it that he has said it to every one of you—that Christianity is splendid, superb, for the hereafter, but a very unhandy and difficult and embarrassing and weighty thing for this present life.

On the other hand, Jesus comes saying that the sane life, the normal life, the real life, the life which is life indeed, is the life changed and filled and controlled by the will of God. Jesus comes with His glorious gospel and gives the right values to life all about us. He comes saying: "I am come to give you life, and to give it more abundantly. I am come to give you freedom that is worth while." Every man serves some master. If that master be not God then it is some master who will do us hurt and make the way difficult and distressing for us. Jesus comes saying: "If the Son, God's Son, therefore, shall make you free, you shall be free indeed." He comes to give freedom. He comes to give fulness of life. He comes to give sanity of life. He comes to conserve life. He comes to ennoble and dignify and glorify life. A man misses the purpose of his creation if he be out of harmony with God. A man does violence to the program of high heaven for him, if he turns away and seeks to give God some remote or small or secondary place in his thinking and in his doing. Jesus comes saying that the supreme thing for a lawyer, or physician, or teacher, or merchant or farmer, or banker, or anybody else and everybody else—the supreme thing to make life sane and balanced and beautiful, to save it, to conserve it, to ennoble it, to glorify it—is Christlikeness.

Oh, that impious fiend from the pit! What artful devices he practices to get the young people, in life's fair morning, with the rainbows of hope spanning all the arches above, to turn away from the highest and best and take the vain, the superficial, the earthly, the evanescent, that which cannot last and which cannot suffice!

The doctrine stated in our text, and emphasized throughout the Bible, that the supreme thing for this present life is that a man should stand beside Jesus, mastered by Jesus, dominated by Jesus, guided by Jesus, sent forth by Jesus, the servant of Jesus, the friend of Jesus, doing His will, and doing it before anything else and before all things else in the world.

Godliness is profitable for this life. In every direction that is true. That is true on every plane where you let your thoughts go. That is true for the human body. The godly man, called to habits of chastity and temperance and purity and cleanliness, called to the task of keeping his body under and his spirit above, ascendant and regal, shares in his body great blessings about which the ungodly man knows nothing. The habits superinduced by godliness make for richness and breadth and fulness and ennoblement of life, even in our bodies. A man is incomparably better off who is the servant gladly and the friend faithfully of Jesus.

Now, that is true also in the great realm of the mind. The devout man, the praying man, the man who desires to know God's mind and to have revealed unto him God's will, that he may follow the same the best he can—that man reaches heights which the prayerless, ungodly man never reaches at all. The man who knows God has a growth and a breadth of mind that the ungodly man can never approach, because a man has entered into the highest realm of all when he has entered into fellowship with God. Oh, how much that means to the student, and how glorious to the student, in the morning of life, to know God, which is the supreme knowledge, the fundamental knowledge. And then when you fight the battles of life, whatever they are, whatever they cost, wherever they lead, the godly man has all the odds in his favor, in the battle of life here and now, for he is rightly positionized toward God. He is right with God. He has said "Yes" to the will of God. He has come under the mastership of God. He yields to the government and guidance of God. Whatever God's will, he says: "I choose that for the law of my life." That man is rightly positionized toward God his Maker, his Master, his Redeemer, his Friend, his Judge. He has made the supreme choice of all. He has committed himself to the all-wise and all-powerful Saviour. Therefore, he can travel life's way with strong confidence in his heart and with a song ringing in every corridor of his being, that all is well. Whatever comes, all is well.

The pivot on which human life in its every deed and thought should turn is this: Am I for Christ or against Him? "He that is not for me is against me; and he that gathereth not with me scattereth." The pivot of life, on which all deeds and words and thoughts and conduct revolve, is the soul's attitude toward Christ. If that attitude be correct, the whole of life is in every way adjusted, and as one goes through the battle of life he meets whatever comes, and he meets it with a victorious spirit. He falls back on that great doctrine, so comforting and reinforcing to the human soul, which says: "We know that all things work together for good to them that love God, to them who are the called according to His purpose." He falls back on the doctrine enunciated in God's Word, that these light afflictions of life, death, sickness, heartache, disappointment, broken plans, overturned ambitions—these light afflictions which are but for a moment—work out for us a far more exceeding and eternal weight of glory. If we truly love God and are the called according to His purpose, we may be vastly fortified by the assurance that the law of compensation will be operative for us. Like a scarlet thread this law may be traced through earth's failures, defeats and tears. If we honestly seek to do God's will here, even though in many respects we fail and taste the bitterness of defeat, still we may know that out there somewhere in God's future the meaning of our tears shall be revealed to us and our seeming failures will be shown to be essential ingredients of ultimate triumph and glory in Christ Jesus.

A man who has settled the question of being for Christ has the right attitude toward God, and then he takes the right attitude toward broken plans, toward everything that comes and goes. Whether for weal or woe, whether draped in black or clothed in white, he takes it all and has the right attitude toward it all. Oh, the importance of the right attitude toward God! A business man is not in a position to live one day through — nor one hour of it, nor one minute of it — if he has not the first question of the human soul rightly settled. He is not in a position to meet any task, to face any experience, to give any decision, like these all ought to be met and given, unless he has the right attitude toward God!

But now our text goes farther than that. It says that this matter of godliness overlaps time, bridges the grave, passes beyond death, sweeps the eternities. Godliness is not only profitable for this life, but profitable also for the life which is to come. How is that so? That is so, first of all, because Christ in His gospel teaches us the clear word about the life to come. Take away the teachings of Christ concerning the life to come, and every scientist and every philosopher and every school man, however clever he may be, is baffled and in the dark concerning the immortality of the soul if you blot out Christ and all His teachings concerning the world to come. Christ comes as the clear teacher setting forth the doctrine of immortality. To man, the creature of time for three score years and ten, may be much less than that — generally so — sometimes a little more than that — Christ comes with His clear doctrine. When the body falls down into dusty death the spirit goes on endlessly in the world beyond, and as are the decisions of the soul this side of the grave so shall be the destiny of the soul beyond the grave. Christ teaches that, the one clear Teacher. That is the teaching of His lips, clear as sunlight. Christ came to bring life and to teach us through His gospel. Caesar speculated, Socrates wondered, Plato queried, and all the rest were utterly at sea concerning that which is beyond death and the grave. Christ comes with His clear word: "I am the resurrection and the life: he that believeth in Me, though he were dead, yet shall be live; and whosoever liveth and believeth in Me shall never die." Fear not them which can kill the body merely. Fear when the killing takes hold also of the soul, the life to come. Christ has taught it and set it all out in its fullness and in its glory. You and I will be out there beyond the sunset and the night, just a little while longer, just a little farther on, in eternity, conscious forever. Christ teaches it. Christ teaches it!

And then Christ teaches that godliness is profitable as we approach the great change, as we come down to the end of the earthly life, and pass through the experience called death, and go across into the world to come. Christ comes to us, His friends, saying: "Give not yourself one moment's uneasiness about that last hour, if you are my friend. Do not be in bondage through fear of death, if you are my friend! To die anywhere, to die at any time, to die in the wreck, to die from the falling building, from the stray arrow, how glorious, how victorious, if you are my friend! To die is gain, if you are my friend. Blessed are the dead who die in the Lord."

He Himself holds you to His own heart. He is your friend, when you come to die. I have buried the past week one who was quite poor with reference to this world's goods, but oh how rich with reference to the graces and victories of the things of God! For some long, long months her illness was something frightful, appalling, even horrible. It was almost imposssible to witness it a half dozen moments, even though one went desiring to be of some comfort and help. And yet in those long months (those who waited by her side said to me) never once did she murmur, and they heard her singing night and day, and she went down into dusty death the past week, chanting that little song:

> Oh, the toils of the road will seem nothing,
> When I get to the end of the way.

And with shoutings, and a change on her face lighting it up with the radiance of the sunlit world, she went away.

> The toils of the road will seem nothing,
> When I get to the end of the way.

Christ gives victory to His friends when they come to die. He guides them out beyond the shadows, out beyond the waiting, out beyond the pain, out beyond the limitations, out beyond the weariness, out beyond all that mars and frightens and distresses, into the richness and fulness which are to be eternal. Oh, we are to be with Christ! That is marvelous — marvelous! To be with Christ! If He were here bodily in the world today, I would want to start before midnight to get to Him. If he were in Palestine, I would want to find Him as quickly as I could. If He were in London, I would want passage on the first boat. If He were in this city tonight in person, and I knew it, not a wink would I sleep until I found Him, if find Him I could. We are to be with Him forevermore, Himself in our midst.

But that is not the best. We are to be like Him. We are to be like Him. All the dross is to be put away. all sins and sinfulness are to be utterly cleansed from us forever. White as the snow, perfected before God, that is the portion of those who in this life intelligently choose Him to be their Saviour and their Lord.

May I ask you a question? Do you want to live the life supremely worth while? Then be for Christ! Great old

Gladstone, just before his home-going in Britain yonder, was approached by one of our American travelers with a question to which the imperial old man made noble answer. The American said, "Mr. Gladstone, what are some of the leading questions now that are agitating England, or should agitate England?" And the grand old man said: "There is but one leading question for England or America, or any other country — just one — and that leading question is for a man to trust his case to Christ as his Saviour, and to go out to live for Christ, whether in Parliament, or on the farm, or wherever life's mission is to be performed."

There is but one leading question, What shall I do with Christ? There is but one leading question, Will I be for Christ? Will I be for Christ? Will I let Him take me and save my life? Forgive my sins first and then save my life? Save it from Satan, save it from hurting people, save it from waste, save it from failure, save it from mistake, and blunder, and perversion, and prostitution, and debauchery, and death? Will I let Christ be my big Brother, and shield me, and guide me, and guard me, and empower me, and save me, soul and body and all? Godliness does that for those who put their trust in Jesus.

Put your trust in Him! O Student, in the morning of life, be for Christ squarely and truly! O young man from the marts of trade, from the walks of business, link your little life with the great Master of Life! O woman, with great capacities for blessedness, for nobleness, for the highest, be for Christ! O stranger within our gates tonight, hear it from a man whose concern is to help your soul: Be for Christ. Be for Him in time, before it is too late, before too much is lost. Be for Him now before the highest and best in you is all maimed and crippled. Give Christ your best of blood, of brain, of manhood, of womanhood, of personality, of influence, of character, of life, of courageous faith. You ought to do that now. Has He spoken to you today? "If you hear His voice, harden not your heart." Has He spoken to you tonight? "Him that cometh to me, I will in no wise cist out." Has the Lord called you tonight? Listen: "Commit thy way unto the Lord; trust also in him; and he shall bring it to pass." He will make your life here and now greater and grander with every rising and setting sun. He will save your life, yourself, now, and you will go to be with Him and to be like Him forever, when you leave the earthly scene and answer His summons: "Come now to be with me." Let us pray.

SERMON VII

The Secret of Contentment

S E R M O N   V I I

The Secret of Contentment

~~~~~~

*I have learned, in whatsoever state
I am, therewith to be content.*
PHILIPPIANS 4:11

PAUL is here praising his fellow-Christians of the church at Philippi for their faithful ministry to him. You will understand that, as he dictates this, he is a prisoner in Nero's dungeon in Rome. He is an old man. The weight of his years and the weight of his tasks are upon him, and he is writing this church, expressing, as only Paul knew how to express, his appreciative regard for their thoughtful remembrance of him through the years.

If you have read Livingstone's tribute to Jesus, you will remember that he crowns it by saying: "Jesus of Nazareth was the finest gentleman that ever lived." And I think David Livingstone would have rated this man Paul as a very high type of gentleman also. Here Paul was dictating to the Philippian Christians sentiments as beautiful as poetry, expressing his appreciation of their thoughtfulness for him and their ministry to him, in the day of his loneliness and confinement and trial.

He did not wish them to misunderstand him. He said: "You will understand that I am not dependent on this. You will understand that I can go on without this. You will understand that I know how to be abased, and I know how to abound. You will understand that these little ministries, these little tokens, these blessed little remembrances that you have sent for my comfort and cheer, while they do cheer me, they are not necessary to me. You will understand

99

that. "But," he said, "I am glad for your sakes that you have done it. I want you to be partners in the rewards that are coming for this great work that we are doing for Christ."

In other words, Paul was saying that he who ministers to Christ's preacher will share in the reward that comes to that preacher's work. He was saying what Jesus had said: "He that receiveth a prophet in the name of a prophet shall receive a prophet's reward." Paul was making the point that the little, modest Christian, can still be the partner of Christ's prophet, as these Philippian Christians had been with him. Paul rejoiced for their sakes, as well as for the sweetness of the pleasure that it brought him, that they had helped him. But then he goes on to declare a great thing when he says: "I am not at all dependent on this. Beautiful as are your messages and your love tokens and your remembrances, I am not at all dependent on this." Then he stated the great text: "I have learned, in whatsoever state I am, therewith to be content."

The Greek word used by Paul which is here translated as "content" means to be master of the situation, to be victor, to be conqueror of circumstances because of the inward sufficiency which was his. What he wrote to the Philippians was something like this: "I have learned in whatsoever state I am, no matter what the circumstances are, to be master of the situation. I have learned to be victor. I have learned to be conqueror of circumstances." These are the ideas that seem to be wrapped up in Paul's statement.

He was a chained prisoner, an old man, suffering in a dungeon. Part of the time he was cold. He wrote one of his comrades: "I wish you would bring my cloak. Sometimes I am cold in this prison; but I have learned, in whatsoever state I am, therein to be independent of circumstances. I have learned that."

To be contented in the sense that Paul meant is one of life's greatest victories. Paul tells us how he got to be such a master when he said: "I have *learned* to be master of my circumstances."

Paul, then, had to learn it. You and I have to learn it. But, surely, it is a lesson supremely worth our learning. Discontent is a miserable spirit. How it must grieve God for men and women to go about moping, miserable, discontented! How that spirit disfigures character! It even disfigures a human face. There are faces that would be handsome, and even beautiful, but for the fact that discontent reigns underneath, like some devouring cancer. And it hurts everybody else for us to go about moping and miserable and discontented! One discontented person in a family can upset the nerves of everybody in the house. One discontented person in the army may impart the mischievous spirit to the whole army. One discontented person in the church of God can perceptibly lower the spiritual temperature of such spiritual family. The friends of God should put away from their minds and hearts the spirit of discontent. They should eschew it utterly. They ought to separate themselves from it.

But it will require much effort. Weeds naturally grow out there in the field. They are indigenous to the field. But if valuable crops or gracious flowers are to grow in the field, there must be cultivation; there effort must be put forth. Weeds will grow in the fields without any plowing or sowing, but great fields of cotton require preparation of the soil, fertilizing, frequent cultivation and much labor. Discontent is a noxious weed. It will grow anywhere. Just let it alone and it will grow. It is indigenous to our nature. We can be miserable, discontented, petulant, impatient, and all that, just naturally; but we are to set ourselves against that. Like Paul we, by practice, by application, by sustained effort, by going to school, are to learn the great lesson of being victor over our circumstances, no matter what they are. We are to learn it. The lessons of life most worth knowing must be learned. We do not wake up some morning suddenly possessed of a superb education. That requires protracted effort, intense application, and concentration. We are to learn this lesson of adequacy in difficulty even as Paul, in his old age, says he had learned it.

We are to learn it by patiently submitting to the inevitable and the unavoidable. Whenever we come to the inevitable and the unavoidable in life, then we are to submit with the right kind of submission and patience. Sooner or later in every human life there comes the inevitable, there comes the unavoidable, and we are to meet it, as Paul met it in the patient spirit of Jesus. Paul was in jail, perhaps chained to another prisoner. He could not help himself. If he moped and worried and fretted and fumed, he would not do himself any good, and he would not do those prisoners any good. Therefore he sang, he dictated great letters to the churches, he preached to those prisoners and some of them were converted, because of the example and the testimony of Paul. He learned how to submit to the inevitable and the unavoidable, and to do it in the spirit of Christ. And this same Paul, in the third chapter of II Thessalonians prayed this prayer for us: "The Lord direct your hearts into the patience which Christ had."

And then again, if we are to learn this great lesson and be master of our circumstances, whatever they are, we must learn how to moderate our desires. Elsewhere Paul says: "Having food and raiment, let us be therewith content." Our desires are to be moderated. Many of us go fuming and fretting and worrying because our desires are abnormal and marked by selfishness. "Having food and raiment, let us be therewith content," says this great workman and witness for God. And you and I are to heed the same lesson. We are to heed it increasingly in these cataclysmic times through which we are passing. Having food and raiment, surely we can be content.

More than that, we can go out with a great, victorious spirit. When we see our young brothers and our sons going out to pour out their lives like water on the field of the world's service, you and I, tarrying at home, can have the spirit of contentment, and of courage, and of song, and of victorious faith that will bear us aloft, no matter what comes. But if we are to have this spirit — the spirit of mastery in all our circumstances, the spirit of victory, no matter what our lot may be — if we are to have that, then we must give our lives to the highest things. Any man who does not give his life to the highest things — namely, Christ's cause, Christ's kingdom, Christ's program — any man who drops below that, who fails to approximate that, shall have his heart torn to shreds with bitterness and disappointment. We are to put first things first. They are the things of the kingdom of Christ. Whatever comes to the world, the kingdom of Christ will emerge victoriously, the will of Christ will be regnant, and the cause of Christ will be standing out there like the great sun in the mid-heaven, whatever comes to the world out of the tragedies — incomparable — through which the world is now passing. And you and I are to put first things first — Christ's will first, religion first, God's Book first, His church first, the kingdom of God and His righteousness first. When we do that, whatever comes we shall be masters of the circumstances that may arise.

Now this truth, dear friends, is to be applied in every position and relation of life. We are to learn how to be masters of our circumstances in any and every relation of life, just what Paul said: "I have learned how to be victor over my circumstances. No matter how black they are, nor how terribly they batter themselves upon me, I have learned how to be victor over my circumstances." We are to learn the same lesson. We are to pay the price to learn it. We are to keep trying to learn it. We are to keep practicing at it. And then we are to apply that principle in every position in human life. We are to apply that principle in the smallest and lowest and most ordinary positions in human life.

103

After you have had a sleepless night, learn how to apply this principle, and learn how to apply it as that sleepless night drags on, and you toss and groan, and wish that your eyes might be heavy, and that your consciousness might be lost sight of in dreamland. Sometimes the slightest thing brings the sleepless night. It is the growling of the cat. It is the barking of the dog. It is the noise of the mouse. It is the crying of some baby. After awhile we are wide awake, and sleep is gone. Let us learn to be master of our circumstances, even when they are like that.

Have you ever read what Emerson says about what to do when you have had a sleepless night? Now, you mark it. He charges you, by all the angels in heaven and earth, if you have had a sleepless night, when you get to the breakfast table not to empty it out on everybody at the table, for you will lower the appetite of everybody at the table, and you will send everybody away from the table to the day's task lowered in power, if you tell at that time the awful night you have had, when this, that or the other thing made it impossible for you to sleep.

And then, when you have read what Emerson says about that sleepless night; turn to Sir Walter Scott's *Journal*, and read what Sir Walter Scott puts down in his Journal: he had set it down as a fixed principle in his life, if he had had a bad night's sleep, or a bad toothache, or a bad indigestion, or a bad anything else, when he got to the table the next morning and met his friends, he would see to it, as a matter of conscience, that they should never know anything about it, so far as he was concerned. That is learning how to be master of our circumstances. Think of a man going to his daily task, doling out his headache, and his toothache, and his earache, and his every other ache, to men and women about him. Who cares? Who cares? Let him keep it all to himself, and be master of his circumstances, be master of his situation.

Paul says: "I have learned how to do that. I have learned how to be self-sufficient. I can go hungry, hungry as the wild beast, and then I know how to eat when they bring food to me. I know how to be abased, and I know how to abound. I have learned how to keep on top of my circumstances."

Apply this principle in the daily task. Apply it in what are called the accidents of life. Read Ralph Connor's book, *Sky Pilot,* and see how the girl Gwynn—impulsive and self-willed, able to ride the horses on the prairies with the speed almost of the wind—met with an awful accident, which crippled that headstrong, restive girl for all her after days. Note her bitterness, her petulance, her impatience, her complaining at the awful lot which had befallen her. Then note that minister who, with careful words, read to Gwynn, talked to her, and explained to her the deep meaning of the mystery of providence in human life. See that minister, as he explains to that restive girl how the great canyon in the mountains came. A mighty upheaval of nature was on and the awful canyon stood out, bald and bare and exposed. Then nature went about the task of putting the beautiful moss all over that gaping canyon, and presently the little flowers came out everywhere, and all that ugly canyon was carpeted with beautiful flowers. By this time the restive and afflicted girl began to see the point: that the upheavals come, and the trials come, and the surprises come, and the reverses come, and the over-turnings of our plans come, but if we will be submissive in the hands of the Great Potter, He will take the canyon and cover it with beautiful mosses, and then cover it with beautiful flowers, and in the place of ugliness He will bring beauty, and in the place of the things that appall He will bring things that entrance and enchant and allure. We are called to make the best of what is called an accident.

I know a woman who has no arms, and yet nobody hears her complain. She has attained considerable distinction as a portrait painter, painting with her feet. Nobody ever hears her complain at all. No arms, but she goes her way songful and victorious from morning to night. And you are thinking of a citizen in our midst who has no arms. Who ever heard him complain? Wherever he goes he is a challenge, he is an inspiration to us all, to hide our miserable aches and pains, and to go on songful and victorious, whatever comes. We are to learn what to do with what are called the accidents of life. We are to learn to be victorious in them and over them and in spite of them, just as Paul said he learned it.

Nor is that all. We are to apply this principle in home life, and it needs to be applied there. The old Spanish proverb is so true, which says: "There is no home that sooner or later does not have its hush." We are to learn how to apply this principle in home life. There is the hush, caused by this, or that, or the other. We are to learn how to be victorious in the home life. When the home has that hush we are to learn how to be victorious there. Sometimes it is an affliction that will not cease, sometimes it is a disappointment that will not change. Sometimes it is this, sometimes it is that, or the other. Paul said: "I have learned how to keep on top, no matter what the circumstances are. I have learned how. I am victor, I am master, I am conqueror, no matter what the circumstances are." Now, we are to learn to do that in home life.

Surely, that is to be learned in married life. Oh, how often separations and disturbances and alienations come because the mind is not fully made up to make the best of it and to say: "I will go my way, saying not a word about it. I will make the best of this." Read the story of Carlyle and his wife. He growled at her, and she growled at him, and the world has the miserable story of their wretched unhappiness in home life. They should not have growled at all; neither of them should ever have spoken of it to anybody else. People ought to learn how, in that sacred relation—for better, for worse, for richer or poorer, till death do us part—to make the best of it all. Oh, that big question of marriage! When will parents be careful enough, and when will young people be careful enough? And then, when that union is effected in the sight of God, calling upon His name to witness and His spirit to bless, the best is to be made of it until the day is done—the best! Learn how to make the best of it.

And then this principle is to be applied universally. Universally we are to make the best of our circumstances. With all our limitations and trials and surprises and reverses, with all the unexpectedness and bitterness of our disappointments, we are to learn how to make the best of it all. Oh, wretched thing, if a man turn cynic! Cynicism takes the wine out of human life, and in its place puts vinegar. A man is in an awful plight, if he allows himself to tread the road of the cynic one second. Whatever the burdens and battles and Black Fridays, whatever the disasters and disturbances and disappointments, a man is to refuse to allow the language of cynicism to enter into his language, provoking him to speak words uncharitable and severe and censorious. Life's wine is turned into poison when mixed with cynicism. Whatever the limitations, whatever the disasters, whatever the difficulties, whatever the burdens, whatever the circumstances, you are to learn how to be victorious in them all, and over them all. Read the life story of John Wesley, that great apostle for Jesus. If he had been alive when Jesus was here, I wonder if Jesus would not have chosen him as one of the twelve. Go and read his life and see how that man was pulled around by the hair of his head by his wife. And yet, in spite of all his domestic burdens, he went on preaching. I am not sure that you or I would have done that, but that is what we ought to have done. Oh, we are to learn how to be master, how to be victor, how to be conqueror. Whatever the circumstances are, whatever the limitations, whatever the difficulties, whatever the battle, learn how to be self-sufficing, to be independent, to be victorious—just what Paul said.

Sometimes the trial will come all unexpected, awful tidings will be announced. It so happens every week even in this fair city. Does the unexpected strike here or there or yonder?

Because God lives and loves, and because He cares, and because our trust is in Him, and because He is our anchorage, and because we believe on Him—whatever shall betide us we believe on Him — we are to be self-sufficient, and go on singing, until the day is done. Bunyan, in Bedford gaol, for twelve long years, put down his lessons and teachings into a book that next to the Bible sways the world. He learned what to do with his circumstances. Now, you are to learn that. When ill health comes, when business reverse comes, when the disastrous surprise comes, you are to get on your feet, and you are to be master of circumstances to the journey's end.

How did Paul win his victory? He won through Christ. Several sentences later in this same chapter he says: "I can do all things through Christ, which strengtheneth me. I can do it because of Christ. He is my dynamic. He is my powerhouse. He is my inspiration. He is my breath of life and power. I can do it because of Christ. I cannot do it in any other way."

I knew a man years ago who was a notorious swearer. His habits were notoriously vicious, but now he is an entirely changed man. I met him the other day and said: "Tell me about it." He said: "I had, you know, a devil of a temper, and my habits, as you know, would put the devil to shame, they were so debased and bad." But now he prays in public, and prays in his family, and his lips do not seem ever to have uttered one polluting word. I said: "Tell me, how did it all happen." And he looked at me and said: "I can do all things through Christ, which strengtheneth me." He can. He could. He did. He does.

Our hope is not a philosophy. Our hope is not an ethic. Our hope is not a creed. Our hope is not a beautiful picture. Our hope is not an ideal. Our hope is in Christ. Jesus will help that little woman, with her big battle at home, to live like she ought to live, if she will lean on Him. He will help that man, cursed with the demon of ambition and envy, cursed with this demon or the other, and will send him down through the streets a victor, if he will lean on Christ.

"I can do it all because of Christ." Do you say that? Won't you say that, and cling to Christ and lean on Christ, and be master because of Christ, and conqueror because of Christ? "More than conqueror," He said, "you shall be, if you will put your whole case in My hands, and go right on doing My will." And then we can wait for it all to be explained, these mysteries, these burdens, these battles, these surprises, these providences. We can wait a little while, and it will all be explained. One of the modern poets expresses it for us in some very simple but pungent lines:

> Sometime, when all life's lesson have been learned,
>   And sun and stars forevermore have set,
> The things which our weak judgment here has spurned,
>   The things o'er which we grieve, with lashes wet,
> Will flash before us, clear in life's dark night,
>   As stars shine most in deeper tints of blue,
> And we shall see how all God's plans are right,
>   And what seemed most reproof was love most true.
>
> And we shall see how, while we cry and sigh,
>   God's plans go on, as best for you and me,
> And how He heeded not our feeble cry,
>   Because unto the end His eyes could see.
> And e'en as prudent parents disallow
>   Too much of sweet to craving babyhood,
> So God perhaps is keeping from us now
>   Life's sweetest things, because it seemeth good.
>
> And if sometime, commingled with life's wine,
>   We find the wormwood, and rebel and shrink,
> Be sure a wiser hand than yours or mine
>   Pours out the potion for our lips to drink.
> And if some friend we love is lying low,
>   Where human kisses cannot reach his face,
> Oh, do not blame the Loving Father so,
>   But wear your sorrow with obedient grace.

And you shall shortly know that lengthened breath
  Is not the fairest gift God gives His friend.
Sometimes the sable pall of death
  Conceals the sweetest boon God's love can send.
If we could push ajar those gates of life
  And stand within, and all God's workings see,
We could interpret all this doubt and strife,
  And for each mystery could find the key.

But not today. Then be content, poor heart.
  God's plans like lilies pure and white unfold.
We must not tear the close shut leaves apart.
  Time will reveal the calyxes of gold.
And when through patient toil we reach yon land,
  Where tired feet, with sandals loosed, may rest,
Where we shall clearly know and understand,
  I'm sure that we will say: "God knoweth best."

Let us pray.

SERMON VIII

A Prayer for Patience

S E R M O N   V I I I

A Prayer for Patience*

~~~~~~

> *The Lord direct your hearts . . .*
> *into the patience of Christ.*
> II THESSALONIANS 3:5.

OUR text this hour calls us to think together on one of Paul's most impressive prayers: "The Lord direct your hearts . . . into the patience of Christ." You will note that I am quoting from the Revised Version, in this sentence, which brings out the meaning of the text more clearly and accurately than does the old version.

If ever there was a timely prayer for us all and each, surely it is this prayer that Paul prays: "The Lord direct your hearts into the patience of Christ." The call to patience is everywhere magnified in the Bible. Again and again, its writers summon us to patience, to patient continuance in well doing. The Apostle James thus calls us: "Take, my brethren, the prophets, who have spoken in the name of the Lord, for an example of suffering affliction and of patience. Behold, we count them happy who endure. Ye have heard of the patience of Job, and have seen the end of the Lord, that the Lord is very pitiful and of tender mercy." And thus does Jesus admonish us: "In your patience, ye shall win your souls."

Every step of the earthly life needs to be fortified with patience. It is one virtue needed by everybody, always and everywhere. The child in school constantly needs this virtue of patience, or he or she will not properly learn. The boy on

---

*Reprinted by permission of the Sunday School Board of the Southern Baptist Convention, from *Follow Thou Me.*

the playground needs it, or his play may easily be turned into a curse. The mother in the home needs it, every hour, with her never-ceasing duties toward her growing children. The father constantly needs it, as he fares forth to grapple with the duties and burdens of his daily work and warfare. The worker in every realm is in constant need of patience. The preacher surely needs this virtue in a large degree, or he will be tempted to resign about once a week. So important is patience that it is not to be wondered that Jesus said: "In your patience, ye shall win your souls."

Often the finest natures are sorely tempted to exhibitions of impatience, just as the fairest lakes of Scotland are often swept by unexpected storms. Think of Moses, meekest of men, so losing his patience that he shattered the tables of the law. Think of Simon Peter who allowed himself to get into such a temper that he angrily cut off the ear of one of the high priest's servants. The Great Master reminded him: "Put up again thy sword into its place; for all they that take the sword shall perish with the sword." Verily, the finest, noblest natures are often tempted to pitiful exhibitions of impatience. Certainly, our text this hour is a suitable and necessary prayer for every one of us. Let us pray it, unceasingly, even that the Lord will ever direct our hearts into the patience of Christ.

The text directs our attention to the one perfect pattern of patience. That pattern is Christ. The patience of Christ, like all of His other virtues, is perfect. We are to keep on looking unto Him, as our example, as well as our Saviour and Lord. We are to walk in His steps. We are to be imitators of Him.

See Christ's patience in dealing with His own disciples. They were ignorant; they learned His teaching slowly; they were, at times, distressingly selfish, and yet, He was sublimely patient through it all. One of them said unto Him: "Lord, show us the Father, and it sufficeth us," to which He made the revealing reply: "Have I been so long time with you, and yet hast thou not known me, Philip? He that hath seen me hath seen the Father, and how sayest thou then, Show us the Father?" On another occasion, two of His disciples selfishly and ambitiously insisted that they be allowed to sit, one on His right hand, and the other on His left hand, in His kingdom. How slow they were to comprehend the spiritual nature of His kingdom, and yet how patient He was with His dull and selfish disciples.

See His patience with the people who pressed upon Him from every quarter for His help. Wherever He went, the multitudes followed Him and found Him. He could not be hid. Toward all who thus sought His help, He was infinitely patient. The most beautiful portrait given of Him in the New Testament is in the five brief words: "He went about doing good." His constant attitude toward the people was that of overflowing helpfulness. His actions ever glorified His words: "The Son of man came not to be ministered unto but to minister, and to give His life a ransom for many." Graciousness, kindliness, active helpfulness toward others marked all the earthly steps of Jesus.

His patience toward His foes was still more wonderful. They sought to circumvent His plans and to frustrate His work, whichever way He went, but His patience was undimmed and undiminished through it all. Nor was His patience the patience of weakness. He reminded His opposers that He could call upon His Father and secure more than twelve legions of angels to come to His aid, if He so desired. But that procedure would have been out of harmony with both His spirit and His plans.

Nor was His patience the patience of Stoicism. There was never another so sensitive as He, or who felt so keenly the sins and woes of earth. Nor was His patience the patience of sullenness, like that of some savage who sometimes bears torture in grim silence. Never in all the world, before or since, has any other shown patience so gracious and gentle

115

and enduring. He prayed for His murderers, and gave back gentlest answers to most cruel words, and then endured His lonely, cruel cross and died thereon for us all.

Mark also His patience with His work. He saw few visible results to His work, while He was here in the flesh. He was a sower rather than a reaper. Great multitudes followed Him at first, but under His winnowing words, they kept falling away from Him, until one day He put the surpassingly pathetic question to the twelve: "Will ye also go away?" Still, He never faltered but went steadily on and on, unwavering and undiscouraged. He fulfilled the prophecy of Isaiah: "He shall not fail, nor be discouraged."

Note again His sublime patience in accepting His Father's will. Listen to His blessed words: "My meat is to do the will of Him that sent me, and to finish His work." And again: "The Father hath not left me alone, for I do always those things that please Him." He accepted His Father's will, even as you and I are to accept it, in Gethsemane, as well as when all life's conditions are cloudless and filled with music. In dark Gethsemane, He prayed: "O my Father, if it be possible, let this cup pass from Me; nevertheless, not as I will, but as Thou wilt." That is to be our prayer as well as His. Have we learned the deep secret of abiding, satisfying peace? Where is it to be found? It is found in the unreserved acceptance of God's will. Why should we be afraid to accept His will for our lives? His will is always right, and always best, and always safe. To go against His will is to invite certain disaster for ourselves. Van Dyke voiced this great truth for us, in his poem. Let us note well its message:

> With eager heart and will on fire,
>   I sought to win my great desire:
>   Peace shall be mine, I said, but life
> Grew bitter in the endless strife.
>
> My soul was weary and my pride
>   Was wounded deep, to heaven I cried,
>   'God, give me peace or I must die'—
> The dumb stars glittered no reply.

Broken at last, I bowed my head,
  Forgetting all myself, and said,
  'Whatever comes, God's will be done,'
And in that moment peace was won.

But let us faithfully note that there was one thing of which Jesus was sublimely impatient. He was impatient of evil, of unrighteousness, of sin. "To this end was the Son of God manifested, that He might destroy the works of the devil." Go read Christ's sharp denunciation of the Pharisees and the Sadducees, and mark His sublime impatience toward their grievous sins. It is the duty of nobody to be patient when evil is to be checked and when wrong is to be righted. It is the duty of no man to be a martyr when he ought to be a soldier. All our liberties in America were won by heroic impatience against tyranny. Where would religion have been in Scotland, if Knox had trifled? What would have become of the Christian faith, in Germany and in Europe, but for Martin Luther? Where would the cause of missions have gone, but for William Carey? What would have become of civilization in recent years, if autocracy had not been summoned to answer at the bar of public opinion throughout the earth? Both in church and in state, in the kingdom and in the commonwealth, we are continually summoned by the most commanding motives of life, to be ever aggressively impatient against wrong ideals and standards, and for the right, throughout the social order, everywhere. Morning, noon and night our prayer is to be: "The Lord direct our hearts into the patience of Christ."

All the relations of life continually call for this virtue of patience. We need patience with and for ourselves. Jesus reminds us: "In your patience, ye shall win your souls." The earthly life is a constant battle. Sore temptations confront us, whichever way we turn. These temptations come to us, as they did to Jesus in the wilderness, in every adroit and specious form. We are to repel them as Jesus repelled them. It is never right to do wrong. To be misled by the subtle doctrine, that "the end justifies the means," is to be led into inevitable defeat and distress. The one canon of conduct, from which we are never to swerve is this: "What is right?" We are to follow the behest of right, if the heavens fall. Thus does the poet put it:

> If thou canst plan a noble deed,
> And never flag till it succeed,
> Though in the strife thy heart must bleed;
> Whatever obstacles control,
> Thine hour will come, go on, true soul,
> Thou'lt win the prize, thou'lt reach the goal.

Not only do we need patience with ourselves, but we need it poignantly in all the relations of life. We need it in our constant contacts with our fellow humanity. It is needed every day and hour, in the most important circle of all—the home. Everyone should continually live at the highest and best in home life. To do so, a large measure of patience will be indispensably necessary. Parents need this grace in abundant measure, as they deal with their eager, growing children. And, surely, the children need it every hour, or they will fall short of their duties toward their parents and toward everybody else. Likewise, this grace of patience, wise and worthy patience, is immeasurably important between husbands and wives. A husband and wife were impatient, each toward the other, ere he left for his office, one early morning. Sharp words were exchanged between them, and in that unhappy temper, they went their separate ways for the day. Alas! A fatal accident came to him during the day and his lifeless body was brought back in the evening to the unhappy home of the morning. Another couple went their separate ways in the morning, each to their waiting tasks of the day, but not until each one had told the other again, the old, old story of ever-growing confidence and love. The second husband's lifeless body was also brought back home in the evening, but the wife's memories of their last conversation and parting, in the morning, will make music in her heart forever. Oh, what need for patience, thoughtful and unceasing patience, in every home in the world, and to the end of day!

Then, too, a large measure of patience is constantly needed in all our contacts with our fellow humanity. Not all persons are reasonable and congenial. Some are very exacting and unreasonable. Even the mighty Paul prayed to be delivered from unreasonable and wicked men. Unless we have a right measure and a proper use of patience we shall sorely misunderstand and misjudge our fellow humanity. If we knew all the background in other people's lives, our judgment of them would be different, our attitude toward them would be changed.

Let me illustrate with a frequently recited story, in connection with the widely famed evangelist, Sam Jones. The last time that I heard him speak, he was pleading, even as I have been pleading this hour, that we all make much of the grace of patience in our relations toward all mankind. To give emphasis to his contention, he told of a day's travel, some months before, through a desert country, one sultry summer day. The train windows could not be kept up, because of the blinding dust, nor could they be kept down, because of the oppressive heat. The day's travel was exceedingly trying for all the passengers. When the nightfall came, the desert had been crossed, and a sleeping car was added to the train. The tired passengers hastened to find rest and sleep after their unusually trying day. At one end of the Pullman car, a man was seen with a tiny baby in his arms, which baby he was vainly trying to quiet. The more he strove to quiet the fretting child, the louder became its cries. Tired men turned uneasily in their berths. Presently, a big, brawny fellow impatiently called to the man who was vainly trying to quiet the crying child: "Why don't you take that baby to its mother?" There was a moment's pause, and then came back the reply: "The baby's mother is in her casket in the baggage car ahead!" Again, there was an awful silence for a moment, and then the man who asked the cruel question, was out of his berth, dressed himself rapidly, and hastened to the man with the motherless child, to make his worthiest apology for his thoughtless question. The father of the child was entreated to get some sleep, while the thoughtless questioner gave himself for hours to the task of quieting and caring for the little one. How easy it is to misunderstand and to misjudge our frail, fellow humanity! More and more, let us magnify a wise and worthy patience, in all our contacts with them.

Most of all, we need patience with God. Let us say it very humbly and reverently—we need patience with God. His providential dealings with us are such as must often try our hearts to the depths. Sometimes our most cherished plans are broken into shreds. Sometimes we are turned utterly away from the things upon which we have set our hearts. Paul essayed to go into Bithynia, but the Holy Spirit would not suffer him to do so. Instead, Paul was directed to Europe, and because he went to Europe, blessings immeasurably vast have come to the world. God's plan for Paul's life was far larger and better than Paul's plan for himself. God's plan for us is always best for us, whatever His plan may be, and wherever it may lead. Ever and forever, we are to say with Job: "Let come on me what will, though He slay me, yet will I trust in Him."

As we travel on let us ever remember that Christ's gospel is the supreme friend of patience, in two ways. First, because love is the supreme thing in life. "Love never faileth." What makes a mother patient with her duties in the home, exacting and endless? It is love. What was it that enabled Jacob to toil for seven arduous years, and then for another seven years? It was his love for Rachel. What is the very heart of the glorious gospel of Christ? Paul states it for us: "The life which I now live in the flesh, I live by the faith of the Son of God, who loved me and gave Himself for me."

Again, Christ's gospel is the supreme friend of patience, because of the immortal hope that it ever holds up before us.

120

The noble old Hebrews called often to mind the saying: "Let Jerusalem come into your mind." Jerusalem was the glorious Hebrew city of old. There they had their noble Temple, with all its traditions and historic glory. No matter, therefore, how far the ancient Hebrew wandered from the ancient city, the old saying, "Let Jerusalem come into your mind," would ever thrill the Hebrew heart. Even so, as we journey on, we are often to let the Immortal Hope and the Eternal Home come into our minds, and thus shall we be the better fortified for the battles and burdens of the earthly journey. "Let not your heart be troubled—in my Father's house are many mansions—I go to prepare a place for you—and if I go and prepare a place for you, I will come again and receive you unto Myself, that where I am, there ye may be also."

In his very human poem, *A Life Lesson,* James Whitcomb Riley voices our undying hope:

> There! little girl; don't cry!
>   They have broken your doll, I know,
> And your tea-set blue, and your playhouse too,
>   Are things of the long ago;
> But childish troubles will soon pass by—
>   There! little girl; don't cry!
>
> There! little girl; don't cry!
>   They have broken your slate, I know;
> And the wild, glad ways of your schoolgirl days,
>   Are things of the long ago;
> But life and love will soon come by,
>   There! little girl; don't cry!
>
> There! little girl; don't cry!
>   They have broken your heart, I know;
> And the rainbow gleams of your youthful dreams,
>   Are things of the long ago;
> But heaven holds all for which you sigh,—
>   There! little girl; don't cry!

That one sentence, "But heaven holds all for which you sigh," forecasts the whole vast story of the glorious life and land beyond, for the true friends and followers of Christ.

121

> We'll gather broken threads again,
> And finish what we here began;
> Heaven will life's mysteries explain—
> And then, ah, then we'll understand.

What then is the way of wisdom for us all? It is that we shall take two worlds into account. "Godliness is profitable unto all things, having the promise of the world which now is, and of that which is to come." We are citizens of two worlds—let us wisely live for both. Let us trustfully link our lives with Christ, faithfully following wherever He leads, and then shall all be well with us, both here and hereafter.

> Lord, I would clasp Thy hand in mine,
> Nor ever murmur, nor repine,
> Content, whatever lot I see,
> Since 'tis my God who leadeth me.

SERMON IX

A Living Sacrifice

S E R M O N   I X

A Living Sacrifice

~~~~~~

> *Present your bodies a living sacrifice.*
> ROMANS 12:1

YOU will generously allow me to take a moment or two to voice brief personal expressions before coming to my message. First of all, I would voice my inexpressible gratitude to God and to you for all the privileges and blessing that have been mine through these forty years of fellowship with this congregation and with the people of this blessed community. When I came to you forty years ago, you received me without the knowledge that is supposed to come with age and without the wisdom that is supposed to come with experience. You took me as I was. The embarrassments must have been many to you because of my limitations and frailties and mistakes. Through it all your patience and forbearance have been unfailing. The overflowing gracious consideration of the church for the pastor and his family has been to us an ever-increasing wonder.

And your practical, steady, unwavering cooperation with respect to the great cause to which the church is inviolably committed has been a joy that would turn the darkest hour into morning for the pastor.

This church is vitally bound up with great causes. All causes fostered by our beloved denomination are immeasurably dear to the heart of this church. Deeply entrenched in our hearts are Buckner Orphans Home, Baylor Hospital, the Relief and Annuity Board, the Baptist Standard—all located here in Dallas. Our devotion is also given to the Seminary at Ft. Worth, Baylor University and our other blessed schools in Texas. These educational institutions deserve and receive our wholehearted support. The church never wavers in its generous and prayerful support of the glorious work done by our State Mission Board, the Home Mission Board and the Foreign Mission Board. We count it a high duty and privilege to give our support to every great and worthy cause fostered by our beloved denomination.

Your pastor's heart ever rejoices in the fact that this church unceasingly and fervently gives itself to the main business of a church of our Lord Jesus Christ which business is the winning of souls from darkness to light, from the bondage of Satan to the liberty of salvation through Christ. This indeed is the primary, preeminent, supreme cause. Let us ever major on the main task. The church secretary reminds me that since I came here forty years ago over 16,000 persons have joined this church; that the pastor has baptized several thousands of them; and that a steady stream has gone out from this church to suburban churches all through the city and the churches farther and farther away, even to the outposts of the nation. I am at home in any community now in America, because some former member of the First Church comes up to bid me welcome. Here indeed is a city set on a hill. Here is a light which is not under any bushel.

And your giving has been steadily deepening and increasing. I think you realize that God's favor cannot be upon a church of miserly people. Stinginess is a direct denial of the Christian faith. I thank God for the liberality and generosity of the people of this church.

Since you gave earnest attention to this great church plant covering the whole block, and some eighteen months ago said, "Let us reduce the large indebtedness thereon," you have laid over $100,000 on the altar for that cause.* All of this is sweeter than the honey in the honeycomb to the heart of the pastor of this church.

---

*Editor's Note: The entire indebtedness on the church was paid —well in advance of due date—before his homegoing, July 7, 1944.

In Psalm 31 David exclaims in an eventful hour of his life, "Blessed be the Lord: for He hath showed me His marvelous kindness in a strong city." That is my cry today: "Blessed be the Lord: for He hath showed me His marvelous kindness in a strong city." My heart says, day and night, what Paul said: "I am a citizen of no mean city." I have said around the encircling globe that there are more forward-looking men and women in this city, proportionately, than in any city I know of in the world.

Today we take one brief glance backward, and then set our faces to the days ahead. I believe with Browning that "the best is yet to be." I believe that the great victorious days of the church are not in the past but that they are in the future. Not a doubt have I of it, provided we are faithful to the Word and to the work of Christ. God has made us trustees of a most solemn and commanding trust. Not a doubt have I that the most blessed days of our dear church are not in the yesterday gone, but in the unfolding tomorrow toward which we turn our faces.

And now, turning away from these personal expressions, let us think together for a little while today on the simple but very vital theme, "The Dedication of Life to Christ and His Cause." I desire on this anniversary Sunday to focus your attention on some words of Paul found in the twelfth chapter of his letter to the Romans: "That ye present your bodies a living sacrifice, holy, acceptable unto God, which is your reasonable service." There can be no substitute for the dedication of self to Christ. "I seek not yours but you," is ever the Master's quest. "If any man would save his life, he shall lose it; but if any man would lose his life for my sake and the gospel's, the same shall save it." These words of Jesus forever stand true.

Our scripture reading for today tells of David going into the house of God with a burnt offering to pay his vows. References to burnt offerings are found all through the Old

127

Testament. Always, in the Bible, burnt offerings symbolize the dedication of life. That is the significance of the sentence we find in II Chronicles 29:27 which says: "When the burnt offering began, the song of the Lord began, also." This is the record of a spiritual revival in the days of good King Hezekiah. He was, as you know, one of the best kings of the Old Testament, even as his father, Ahaz, was one of the worst. Satan often outwits himself. The riotous wickedness of Ahaz, the father, seems utterly to have repelled Hezekiah, the son. Satan is clever, quite clever, but he often outwits himself and one day will be outwitted utterly and forever, and chained in everlasting darkness where he belongs. Now, when young Hezekiah came to the throne, his behavior was nobly praiseworthy. He found conditions very bad—socially, governmentally, religiously, every way; but his brave young heart did not quail. He lost no time temporizing by parleying.

Just here a good many persons, we may well fear, completely lose out. They face a great matter of right or wrong and they parley before it, they temporize with it and, alas, often they compromise concerning it. There are times when those two little words "yes" and "no" are to be said without one moment's hesitation and with all positiveness.

When young Hezekiah came to the throne, his first act as king was notably significant. He gave religion the first place in his kingdom. Woe betide any country that does not. Woe betide the rulers of a country that do not. He gave religion the primacy in the life of his nation. The temple doors had long been closed by the edict of the wicked father. The people were denied the privileges of worship, as they are in some quarters of Europe now, as I have seen with my own eyes. The doors were closed in their faces. They were barred from the privileges of worship through the edict of Ahaz, the wicked king. But the noble young king, as his first kingly act, opened the doors of the temple of worship. He called the people back to sing their praises and to offer their worship to the living God. The young king wisely recognized that all abiding prosperity of a country runs its roots down deep into religion. It is utterly useless to try to mend a country's distress if we ignore morality and religion. The first, the last and supreme line of defense for a country is not financial and material but moral and spiritual.

> Ill fares the land, to hastening ills a prey,
> Where wealth accumulates and men decay.

Blessed is that nation whose God is the Lord. This young king realized what rugged old Carlyle repeatedly said, namely: "Religion is the determining factor of any and every civilization." And when Carlyle said it he was echoing the Bible which says, "Righteousness exalteth a nation but sin is a reproach to any people." The young king realized that he and the people had sinned and that they were straightway to confess their sins to God and seek His mercy. Accordingly, a beast was chosen from the field, called a sin offering, as was the custom of the early day. And when the beast was brought as a sin offering, young Hezekiah humbly and penitently confessed his sin, and the people followed in his train confessing their sin, and the beast was led away and put to death. That solemn ceremony typified the coming sacrifice of the Son of God, who came down from heaven and after a little journeying here, climbed his lonely cross and died thereon, the just for the unjust, that He might bring us to God. And, therefore, we sometimes sing:

> My faith would lay her hands
> On that dear head of Thine,
> While like a penitent I stand
> And there confess my sin.

The young king led the way in the confession of sins and the people followed him. Wouldn't you like to see all the kings and presidents and rulers of the world one time down on their knees sincerely confessing their sins to Almighty God?—and they have plenty to confess! Wouldn't you delight one time to see them like that? Then surely the people would be swept with a tumult of emotion and they would be constrained by a drawing power such as the world has never seen on so vast a scale. If only we could see that!

The young king realized that the one abominable thing which God hates is sin. He realized the truth of the word of God: "Your sin has separated between you and God." Sin in a veil through which we cannot see God. Sin is an insulator that cuts off the current between God and us. "Blessed are the pure in heart for they shall see God"—see Him here and now as well as in the world to come. "Who shall ascend into the hill of the Lord and who shall stand in his holy place? He that hath clean hands, and a pure heart; who has not lifted up his soul unto vanity, nor sworn deceitfully. He it is that shall receive the blessing of the Lord." "If I regard iniquity in my heart, the Lord will not hear me."

Oh, if this nation, and the other nations as well, would come in the spirit of this great Bible truth, what a change the world would experience in one brief hour. "If my people, who are called by my name, shall humble themselves, and pray, and seek my face, and turn from their wicked ways; then will I hear from heaven, and will forgive their sin, and will heal their land." A nationwide revival of real repentance toward God because of sin, a world-wide revival of that sort, would have hushed wars of every kind to the ends of the earth and would carry the Kingdom of God forward like the swelling tides sweep the seas again and again.

But after that sin offering, then what? The cleansing comes, for God hears the penitent's prayer, He forgives those who repent of their sins. He delights to answer the publican who cries, "God be merciful to me a sinner." He delights to answer the cry of the penitent sinner. King and people have been forgiven. Now they stand in the sunlight of God's grace. What shall they do now? In the olden times there was another offering brought, that was the burnt-offering. And, I repeat, it always stands in the Bible for the dedication of life. "Now

130

when the burnt-offering began, the song of the Lord began, also."

Now we are in a position to understand Paul's great word: "That ye present your bodies a living sacrifice, holy, acceptable unto God, which is your reasonable service." When that burnt-offering began the shadows lifted, the clouds dispersed, the sunlight came again, music spread through all the air, joy and rejoicing were in the hearts of the people. Now in that ancient and dramatic scene there are vital lessons for us; and the New Testament picks up the idea of the burnt-offering, of the dedicated life, and gives it an emphasis which ought to appeal to all our hearts. "I beseech you therefore, brethren, by the mercies of God, that ye present your bodies a living sacrifice, holy, acceptable unto God, which is your reasonable service." You belong to Christ by virtue of a three-fold claim. You are Christ's by creation, He made you; you are His by redemption, He died for you; you are His by preservation, He supports and preserves you. Therefore present your bodies, dedicate your bodies, a living sacrifice, holy, acceptable unto God, which is your reasonable service.

Herein are numerous lessons for us. But we have time today for just one. Whenever life is dedicated to a cause that cause is likely to be carried forward. Wherever a life is really, fully, unreservedly, persistently dedicated to a cause, that cause is likely to be carried forward triumphantly. If a man withholds himself from a cause, it he touches it just as lightly as he can, if he gets by it the easiest way he can, it will be very bad for him and worse for the cause. This explains why many men fail. They touch their problems in life with timid fingers; they throw down their tools at the first sound of the bell. Their hearts, their deepest loyalties and loves, their highest devotions are not put into the cause at all. You can apply this principle universally. Let a student take hold of his studies just a little bit, just barely enough to pass, the chances are that he will go limping down the years greatly handicapped by the lack of worthy preparation. If a man goes to his work counting the hours and minutes until the dinner bell sounds, and drops the ax or hoe or pen with the first note of that bell, and scampers away to get his dinner, and tarries until the last note of the bell calls him back, it is bad for the cause and bad for him. But if a man will put himself into his business and make himself indispensable to it, the chances are that one day he will own that business, he will be its directing head.

Apply this principle to the bearing of life's burdens and crosses. Sooner or later they come to all of us. "In the world ye shall have tribulations," said Jesus. How do we relate ourselves to our burdens and crosses when they come? If we rebel, if we mope, if we complain petulantly, if we whine from morning until night under it, then the burden will grow heavier every day and the hardness of our heart will be deepened every hour. But if, like Job advises, we keep looking for the bright light on the cloud, we shall find it. Every cloud has its silver lining. How do we meet life's burdens, life's sorrows, life's crosses? If we are meeting ours like Paul met his, then victory lies ahead. Though Paul be in jail he would start a prayer-meeting and the jailer would come crying out: "What must I do to be saved?" Bind Paul with chains in Nero's prison, and he will write to the Philippians saying: "Rejoice in the Lord, and again, I say, rejoice. . . . I would have you understand, brethren, that the things which have happened unto me have fallen out rather unto the furtherance of the gospel."

Because he fully dedicated himself to Christ and His cause, Paul could say: "I have learned, in whatsoever state I am, therein to be content." There is much wisdom in the old saying, "Make the best of it." Have you a burden, domestic, social, financial, physical? "Make the best of it." God is on His throne. He lives and loves and cares. He is not unmindful of what you are passing through. Make the best of it. Turn it to the highest account. Lovely Helen Keller did this and called forth the admiration of the world. Make the best of the home trial.

I think there is nothing in history more touching than the behavior of Charles Lamb, the brilliant British essayist and critic, who devoted his best hours to his sister, Mary, who had recurring spells of insanity. Charles Lamb could soothe her into sanity as nobody else in the world could. She adored her brother. He was to be seen many times in the morning, err the sun came up, traversing the lanes of England, talking with Mary, telling her about the singing birds, and the smiling flowers, seeking to keep back that encroaching wave of insanity as it persisted in coming again and again. Glorious!

There were two great writers, each man very able; but how different they were in spirit! One was bitter, cynical, sour, morose. The other never had a word of that anywhere in his writings. The one was Lord Byron, crippled, bitter, rebellious, all the while cynical. Listen to him:

> My days are in the yellow leaf,
>   The flowers and fruits of love are gone,
> The worm, the canker, and the grief
>   Are mine alone.

Poor pitiful Byron! The other was Sir Walter Scott. He said, "I never wrote one line to belittle man in his religious faith, never. I never wrote one line to put bitterness in any man's heart, never." Do you wonder that multitudes bow at the shrine of Sir Walter Scott?

Let us remember that the principle of compensation runs all through life, so that if we lose out here, we make up over there. Emerson's greatest essay is on "Compensation." And he borrowed the main thought of that essay from Paul, where Paul says, "For our light affliction, which is but for a moment, worketh for us a far more exceeding and eternal weight of glory."

Now let us apply this principle a moment or two to the highest realm of all, the realm of religion. "That ye present

133

your bodies a living sacrifice, holy, acceptable unto God." To be acceptable unto God, what does Christ say? He says: "Thou shalt love the Lord thy God with all thy heart, with all thy soul, with all thy mind, with all thy might, . . . and thy neighbor as thyself." This indeed is the devoted, abandoned, dedicated life. Let a man withhold himself from God's great cause and the cause will suffer, it will be misunderstood and misrepresented if such shall be the behavior of the professing friend of Christ. In effect, Christ says to each of us: "I want your life, your personality; I want your manhood; I want your womanhood; I want your social gifts and graces, O women. I want your strong, earnest, heroic work, O men. I want you. I want you at your maximum. I want you fullfledged and four-square in my kingdom. I want you, you in all the magnitude of your capacities."

How many men and women do you think are giving their maximum strength to our Lord? How many do you know? Here is the acid test. Christ asks for our lives. The rich young ruler could not meet the test. Jesus said to him: "If you really are in earnest, you may have eternal life. Go sell your property and give the proceeds to the poor, and come, take up your cross and follow me." But the young man turned sorrowfully away. And why did he turn away? Because he could not make the sacrifice which Jesus asked of him. By his action he said: "The Master asked me to give Him the first place and put my money in the second place. I can't do that. My money comes first and I can't make the sacrifice." How tragic! Because so many professed friends of Christ follow the example of the rich, gifted and lovable young ruler, the cause of Christ is delayed in its progress and those professed friends of Christ suffer irreparable loss. They miss the golden opportunity to attain unto a blessed immortality.

How different the results when God's people truly dedicate themselves unto Him! Moses turned away from the purple and the crown of the great empire of Egypt and dedicated his life to the liberation of the enslaved Israelites. He brought them out and did much to fashion them into a great people. More than 3,000 years have passed since then but the world still glorifies the name of Moses. The Pharaoh and the kings of his time are forgotten but Moses still lives on because he dedicated himself and his all to the doing of God's will.

Paul and Barnabas hazarded their lives for the name of Jesus. When did we hazard our lives or anything else for the name and the cause of Christ? We are told in the New Testament how the early Christians overcame Satan. We are told that they overcame Satan by the blood of the Lamb. That must ever be one of our conquering weapons. A man has no gospel who mocks the atoning blood of Christ. He has nothing better than a gilded humanitarianism. Without shedding of blood there is no remission. And they overcame Satan by the word of their testimony, and by the fact that they loved not their own lives even unto death. That was their threefold way of triumph. And if we make use of these same weapons we also may be assured of certain victory.

Madame Guyon was entirely right when she said that in the great creative hours of life, we may make more progress, perhaps in one hour, than we have made in twenty-five years before. When are the great creative hours in life? They are when you definitely commit yourself and register your deepest resolve, saying: "Sink or swim, survive or perish, live or die, I abandon myself to this course, to this cause, in complete abandonment, in self-sacrificing loyalty and devotion. Here I take my stand." That means dedication of life.

Lovely Florence Nightingale was asked the secret of her power. She waited a moment and said, "The secret is I work very hard, and I never have refused Christ anything." That kind of dedication will win anywhere in the world. If the members of this congregation would adopt and apply to their individual lives, the principles of the dedicated life and the practices of sacrificial service of Florence Nightingale, then it is no exaggeration to say that mighty streams of redeeming, spiritual power would flow out from this church to all of great Texas and the nation and even unto the ends of the earth. Dedicated lives change things. Oh, such lives are needed now!

There are three great institutions of divine appointment—the home, the state, and the church. God gave them all to us. And they all need our best attention constantly. One of the old prophets was pictured as seeking for a man. What do you want him for, Ezekiel? "I want him to stand in the gap." Why? "I see a crisis coming to our country and I want a man to stand in the gap to avert that crisis." Ezekiel wanted a man to do the kind of thing the heroic men of little Holland did when the raging sea was about to break through the dikes and flood their land. They hurled their bodies into the gaps in the weakened dikes and at the peril of their own lives they held the dikes until repairs could be made to hold back the encroaching flood.

Our need now is men to stand in the gap at home. Fathers who will be the right kind of fathers. Mothers who will be the right kind of mothers. And in the realm of government, we need men who will be the right kind of citizens; not sleepy, apathetic, yawning citizens; men who will see that the right standards are not lowered nor dishonored but are kept floating in the face of every storm in all their glory. Oh, how we need men and women like that in the supreme causes of home and church and state! Yes, desperately we need in the church of the living God, the right kind of men and women, men and women who hold themselves and their all in trust for the welfare of humanity and for the glory of God.

Today on this significant anniversary hour, I am looking backward with heart touched more deeply than word of man or angel could possibly describe, looking backward and seeing how the ranks of those who were here when I began have been thinned down to a dozen or less after forty years; and looking ahead, looking ahead when numbers and numbers of us will pass from the scene in the next twelve months, in all probability. And in another few years, the generation that now knows us will not know us save as we are known by the perpetuity of a fine service in the kingdom and cause of our Lord.

If Christ should come down on this platform in person this morning, I think He would say to the pastor: "You may stand aside now for a little while. I have somewhat I wish to say to this people." Then I think He would lift His hands in blessing and say: 'Peace be unto you." Then He would say, "I now ask you to heed the call of this preacher's sermon, if you would re-dedicate your lives to me. May I have the right-of-way in your lives? May I have the primacy? It will be best for you and yours today and tomorrow and forever. May I have my way with you? Will you dedicate your lives to me? If you are neglecting duty, won't you cease such neglect? If you are holding back from me, putting off your return to me, your surrender to me, won't you end that? May I have my way with you today?" What would you say? Surely you would say, "Here, Lord, I give myself to Thee. 'Tis all that I can do." That is all He asks. But He does ask that. Hear Him today. Heed His call today. Follow Him today, I pray.

There are men and women today in this crowded presence, upstairs and in the room below, who ought to link their lives with the church. My friends, you, of course, can go away from this place without doing that at all. But I do not think that would please Jesus nor help you, nor help anybody else. How much better it will be to make a blessed decision and say: "Today in this hour, trustful and happy, I dedicate my life to Christ to do what he asks at my hands, by His grace." Come then and link your lives anew with Him and His cause in this church. Come with your letters or come upon your statement and we will get your letters; or come upon your open confession of faith in the Christ, to follow Him a little later in beautiful baptism. Come today and make your surrender to Him. Today if you hear His voice, harden not your heart.

Come! Our hearts and hands are open to you in most joyful welcome. Come as we sing:

> I gave My life for thee,
>   My precious blood I shed,
> That thou might'st ransomed be,
>   And quickened from the dead;
>
> I gave, I gave My life for thee,
>   What hast thou given for Me?
> I gave, I gave My life for thee,
>   What hast thou given for Me?

SERMON X

The Christian Optimist

S E R M O N   X

The Christian Optimist

~~~~~~~~~~~~~~~~~~~~~~~~~~~~~~~~~~~~

*But I determined this with myself,
that I would not come again to you
in heaviness.*   II CORINTHIANS 2:1

THE opening sentence of the chapter read to you a few minutes ago is the text for the morning:

"But I determined this with myself, that I would not come again to you in heaviness."

Paul was writing his second letter to the church at Corinth, and he proposed to make a second visit a little later to such church. But he put them on notice that, when he came for this second visit, it would be in a different spirit from that which he had on his first visit. On his first visit he was depressed. Gloom shrouded him. He was down in spirit. His nerves were on edge. He was miserable. He was utterly depressed.

Of course, any preacher with that spirit would impart the same spirit more or less to his auditors. He advised them in this second letter, "When I come next time you need not be afraid that I will act like I did the first time. I have learned better. I have learned that pessimism is worthless. I have learned that gloom clogs and fetters and defeats, and when I come next time I will not come in the spirit of depression which so grieved you when I was with you before." He did not mean to say that there was no occasion for depression and for wringing of heart, for there was such occasion in that church. The church had in it a terrible scandal, and the hearts of the people were greatly distressed.

Oh, is there any other thing that can so break people's hearts as a grievous church scandal? It is next to a family scandal, and the church at last is a big family, a great household. The interests of one are the interests of all. The least is to be looked after and counseled and guarded and loved as well as the greatest.

This church to which Paul was writing this second letter was the scene of a dire scandal, one of the gravest that the whole New Testament mentions. It had thrown the church into a wretched upheaval. The occasion for the scandal—the offender himself, at least—had been thrust from the church, and he was on the outside, but the shame of it all was in the mouths of gainsayers and of scorners there in Corinth. Now, Paul writes, saying: "I recognize all that. I see the weight of all that, but when I come I am determined to look for the bright side. When I was there before, I saw the gloomy side. I saw the clouds; I am coming next time definitely bent on not allowing depression to be the staple of my preaching, to be the note of my testimony. When I come next time I am coming without heaviness at all." He saw the heaviness, the occasion for the heaviness, the occasion for the tears, the occasion for the gloom and depression and sorrow that reigned there in the church at Corinth. He saw it all, but he said: "I am going to look for the bright side, and I will emphasize that when I come back next time."

Now, in that little sentence Paul points a good lesson for every one of us, a lesson which every one of us needs conscientiously to heed, and heed every day. Every human life should have the face always set towards the morning. Optimism should be the reigning habit in every human life. It is difficult for some temperaments to be optimistic, but as a matter of conscience, as a matter of principle, as a matter of duty, as a matter of right, as a matter of wisdom, as a matter of ever-growing happiness and usefulness, every human life should have in it the reigning habit of cheerful optimism. Preachers should have that habit when they deal with their congregations. For my part, I would not want to hear a preacher who had degenerated into a mere scold. I would not hear him. I would find somebody else who had a different message. The teacher should have the reigning habit of cheerfulness as he teaches his pupils, and the physician should have the reigning habit of cheerfulness as he ministers to his patients. The long-faced doctor is the forerunner of the hearse. Certainly the business man should have the reigning habit of cheeerfulness in his life. In fact, that should be the fixed principle of every human life. The face always should be toward the morning. The reasons therefor are weighty and they are evident, if we will pause to think a moment concerning them.

Beginning on the lowest plane, cheerfulness is a duty. Beginning right on the lowest plane, cheerfulness is a duty. There are some duties that must not be ignored by us. It is everybody's duty to be honest. That is everybody's duty. An honest man is the noblest work of God. Everybody's duty it is to be honest. That is fundamental. That goes to the vitals of human life and character and conduct. It is everybody's duty to be clean, to be pure. The unclean, foul life is utterly ignoble and wickedly criminal. It is everybody's duty to be kind. The boor anywhere is an utter misfit, and a most unfortunate creature. It is everybody's duty to be cheerful. That is everybody's duty to be cheerful, constantly cheerful; cheerful, whatever the battle and burden. Whatever the sorrow and suffering, whatever the question and the perplexity, to be cheerful is everybody's duty. We owe that to other people.

All about us there are people fighting their battles, climbing their hills, facing their questions, grappling with their tasks, and we will make their tasks harder if there is absent from our lives the reigning note of cheerfulness. We owe it to every human being about us to go our way singing, even if we have to sing through our falling tears. Cheerfulness is a duty which we owe to other people. You have no more right to unload a nasty temper, a pessimistic, wailing, grumbling temper on your brother or sister—battling alone with big tasks—than you have the right to bring the garbage can and dump its contents on your neighbor's front porch. Bad tempers in the presence of people are bad manners of which no one ought ever to be guilty. It is the quintessence of self-centeredness and self-will and self-preference that you should have a temper that would hurt people and strike them like a blow in the face. Everybody owes it to the people around to exercise the constant habit of cheerfulness.

And then we owe it to ourselves to have that fine habit in our lives. Self-interest calls for it. Well does the Bible say: "A merry heart doeth good like a medicine." A merry heart is a medicine." A merry heart oils the troubled waters of life. We owe it to ourselves to cultivate the merry heart. The man possessed of the most serious life purposes and aims may also be the man of the sunniest soul, if he will take the right view of human life and conduct and character and destiny. A little girl, as she was eating—a tiny little tot she was—as she lifted her spoonful to her mouth saw coming through a place in the window a ray of sunlight, which was focused right on her spoon, as the little thing put it to her mouth, and she exclaimed with a cheery laugh: "Look, I have swallowed a spoonful of sunshine." We ought to swallow spoonfuls every day. Everywhere we go we should scatter sunshine rather than shadows. We owe it to our work. All through it, from early morn till dewy eve, whatever our work, we owe it to our work to oil it with the spirit of cheerfulness. If we go to it like a drudge, if we go to it like a galley-slave chained to his oar, if we go to it with spirits down, if we go to it with a dirge and a wail and a whine, our whole work will be miserable. But if we go to it with a hearty spirit and a brave hand and a fine purpose, bent on being cheerful and optimistic through it all, our work will be a blessing rather than a bane to us.

But, above all else, I come to say that we owe it to God to cultivate the habit of cheerfulness in our lives. Christianity is joyful. "Behold, I bring you glad tidings of great joy," was the announcement the angels brought concerning the babe to be born, the babe to be the world's Saviour. Christianity is joyful. Christianity sees the bright light in the cloud. Christianity always has its face towards the morning. "Rejoice forever more, and again I say, rejoice." That is God's word to us. "Ye are the light of the world." He does not say: "You are the clouds of the world." He does not say: "You are the *night* of the world." Rather, "Ye are the *light* of the world." I feel sometimes that we allow ourselves to be so bedarkened and so cheerless that we can easily give the world about us, unregenerated and lost, the impression that religion is morbid and gloomy and depressing. "Ye are the light of the world." The light of the world! "Let your light so shine that men may see your good works and glorify your Father in heaven."

Do not be like that gloomy aunt, who thought it was a sin to smile, who imagined that she represented religion by being straight-laced and long-faced all the time. When her cheery-hearted niece, a gladsome, natural, human girl, made surrender to Jesus and took her place in the church, as they tell us the story, the girl was human and natural and gladsome after she became a Christian, even more so than before she became a Christian. One day somebody felicitated the aunt because her niece was a radiant Christian. But the aunt slowly shook her head and said: "I am afraid that the work of grace in her is not complete, because she seems to be more addicted to laughter than she ever was before." Do not be like that. That misrepresents God. The sweetest, sunniest, cheeriest, gladdest, most musical, most songful, most rosy-dawned thing in the world, is to be a Christian, to be a wholesome, normal, obedient disciple of Jesus. We are to show the world how music and song and laughter and gladness are a great part of the Christian life.

145

But I invite you to take a step further as I remind you, concerning cheerfulness, that it ought to be in every life. I have said it is a duty, but it is more than that. It is a great privilege. Much of life should be classed as privilege. It is a great privilege to go with sunshine and music and cheerfulness through every experience. Now, that does not mean the absence of seriousness. The man who, in a world like this, is not serious is indeed a strange compound. The man or woman who in this present hour of world testing and world crisis, with the world battle-scarred and war-torn, nobody knowing what the next chapter is to be, the man or woman who is not serious in a time like this—strange and defective is such a person's character.

To be cheerful does not mean we are to take a superficial view of life. If ever there was a man who took a great, deep, masterful, comprehensive view of life, it was Paul. He saw all sides. He saw all conditions and facts. And yet, seeing all, Paul could say: "I have learned that the right spirit, the right temper, the right course, the high privilege, is for a man ever to go singing to his task." A man must not play the ostrich and put his head down in the sand and say: "There are no troubles. There are no sicknesses. There are no sorrows. There is no sin. There is no death." That is madness. Sin is everywhere, and sickness is everywhere, and sorrow is everywhere, and death is everywhere, and clouds are everywhere. But we are to look for the bright light in the cloud. We are to look for the rainbow that spans the dark arch, which rainbow presages certain things that we must not forget. We are to go through life with sunshine and with sweetness, even though often the tears fall.

Paul said in another place: "I have learned in whatsoever state I am therein to be content." And he also said: "In everything give thanks." He did not say, "*For* everything give thanks"; not that. "*In* everything give thanks." In jail he wrote that, with his hands manacled. He said, "I have learned in everything to give thanks."

Whatever comes, whatever the cloud, or the battle, or the sorrow, "in everything give thanks." God can turn the battle back from the gate. He can turn the shadow of death into morning. Give thanks and go on. Cheerfulness is a great privilege, high and holy, as well as a duty.

Cheerfulness is power. A man may be clever; he may be astute in mind. But if he lack the element of cheerfulness, the habit of song in his life, he has missed one of the biggest assets for the battle of life. Cheerfulness is power. If two men are side by side in the same business, and one man be cheerful, with the dawn of the morning on his face and in his works, and the other man be morbid and morose and without smiles, the chances are the first man will soon own both the stores, and the second man will soon be bankrupt. Cheerfulness is a dynamic asset in the big battle of human life. Well does Carlyle say, "Give me the man who sings at his work." On the field of battle, when soldiers are dispirited and dejected and forlorn and down-hearted, and are home-sick and their hearts are poured out like water, we are told that often in one minute they can be galvanized into heroic action, transformed from lambs into lions and be given the spirit of victory, by some great, stirring music. We do well to face our tasks with music in our hearts.

> It's easy enough to be pleasant
>   When life flows by like a song,
>   But the man worth while
>   Is the man who can smile,
>   When everything goes dead wrong.
>
> For the test of the heart is trouble,
>   And it comes with the passing years,
>   And the smile of worth,
>   Winning the prizes of earth,
>   Is the smile that shines through tears.

The lesson I have sought to draw from Paul's decision as recorded in our text does not mean that we are not to see the mountains that have to be climbed. We must see them.

It does not mean that we are not to see the streams that have to be bridged. We must see them. We must see the tunnels that must be digged through the mountains. We must see facts and conditions as they are. And yet, seeing all, we must also seek and find the bright side in every situation. Every human life ought to make the high and infinitely wise resolve which says: "Whatever comes, I am going to live the sunny, cheerful, optimistic, victorious life. Whatever comes, for my own sake, for humanity's sake, for Christ's sake, I am going to travel the road of songfulness and good cheer, clear to the end."

How are we to do that? Let me make two or three simple suggestions. In the first place we must deliberately determine that we will be distributors of sunshine, dispensers of cheerfulness and practitioners of helpfulness all along life's pathway. Let us be convinced of the excellence of that way of life and highly resolve with ourselves that, with God's help, we will walk therein. Determine to be merchants of gladness rather than of gloom. Choose to be wholesale distributors of hope rather than of despair. Such determination, such choice, such resolve is a duty, a privilege and a high commission. It will help to smooth out the rough places in life's pathway not only for our own feet, but also for the feet of many of our fellow pilgrims. It is a good way to become lights of the world and the salt of the earth. Let us therefore irrevocably commit ourselves to the carrying out of the commission of good cheer which Christ gave to all His followers.

In the second place, if we are to abandon the spirit of heaviness, as did Paul, and embrace the habit of helpfulness and good cheer, then must we establish the habit of looking for the bright side in every situation. Every problem, every burden, every task, every experience has two sides—a bright side and a dark side. Even the world war in which we are now engaged has its bright side. It goes without saying that its dark side is exceedingly, horribly dark. The whole world seems to be enshrouded by the black and deadly fumes arising

148

from the pit of destruction. If we see only the dark side of war we should conclude that Hell itself is turning loose its fiercest fury upon the children of men. But for those who have eyes to see and hearts to understand that God can and does make the wrath of men to praise Him, there is a bright side even to war. We must seek and find that side or else this war can result in nothing but despair. It is a terrible tragedy that nations do not learn to settle their differences in other ways than by the instrument of war. It may be that the horribleness of modern warfare will force men, ere long, to substitute the principles and practices of peace and brotherhood for the bloody laws of the jungle. Seen only from its dark side, Sherman was right when he said, "War is hell."

Yes, war always brings forth an abundant crop of evils—tares springing up amid the wheat. But we must not lose sight of the wheat. We must thank God for the wheat, even while we bemoan the presence and the rankness of the tares which flourish in time of war. Even now be can thank God for the display of heroism, the evidences of worthy patriotism, the renewed determinations to preserve the ideals and the blessings of the democratic way of life; for the high resolve that no rampant, aggressive, imperialistic nation shall be allowed to run roughshod over the world. We can and do thank God that multiplied millions of people in our nation and in others of the Allied Nations are willing to sacrifice and suffer and fight and die in order that liberty and freedom and justice and democracy shall not perish from the face of the earth.

Germany and her allies have launched on a program which, if successful, would result in the enslavement of all Europe and ultimately the enslavement of the rest of the world. Such program is not—cannot be—consonant with the will and purpose of God. Therefore, whether we realize it or not, we find ourselves fighting for God and humanity. In the heat and passion and blood and death of this horrible conflict, may the people of these United States not lose sight of God or humanity. If we and our allies can have and hold the vision we shall gain the victory at arms; and, what is infinitely more, we shall help to advance the plans and purposes of God for poor, sinning, suffering, distraught humanity. We are called to a task which is world-wide in its scope and consequences. In proportion as we see and worthily respond to this challenge, this call, this opportunity to serve God and humanity, to that extent will we be serving God's purposes and humanity's needs. All of which is just another way of saying that in whatever circumstances we find ourselves there is always a bright side, there is always a way out, there is ever a victory to be won.

But the main word of all I have yet to say. You cannot see the bright side, you will not find the way out, you will not win the ultimate victory unless you have a power in your life above yourself. Great old Dr. Chalmers had as one of his lofty utterances that expression: "The expulsive power of a new affection." That is what we must have for our great battle in life, every one of us. Every one must have within the expulsive power of a new affection. Love for Jesus is the greatest expulsive power. None, apart from Christ, have moral strength or spiritual resources within themselves sufficient to live life as it ought to be lived. No one has that strength. But Jesus, the Saviour and Guide, the Teacher and Master, the Friend and Helper, comes, saying: "If you will make simple surrender of yourself to me, I will come into your life, and I myself will be the expulsive power of a new affection. If you let me be the Physician and the Master, the Guide and Master of your life completely, by your consent, I will turn your face to the morning. I will fill your lips and heart with songs. I will turn the battle back from the gate, no matter what the battle is."

Oh, my battling, burdened, busy friends, you cannot win in this big game of human life if you do not have Christ in your heart and in your life. But if you will let Him come into your heart, then trustfully, like a little child, say to Him:

"Dear Saviour and Lord, I surrender to Thee. I beseech Thee to pardon my sins and cleanse my soul. I look to Thee for strength and wisdom and victory. I believe that Thou art the divine Son of God and the Saviour of the world. I trust in Thee, and Thee alone, for salvation. I yield myself to Thee, blessed Lord, to be Thy faithful servant. I yield here and now. With Thy help I will follow Thee the rest of the way. I surrender myself and my all into Thy care and keeping for today and forever."

Oh, man or woman, boy or girl, if you will accept and confess Christ in that fashion you can go forth from this place today assured in your heart that you are in the way of victory for this life and for the life to come. You can know that your name is written in the Lamb's Book of Life and that you are made an heir of God and a joint-heir with Christ. Lovingly, tenderly, insistently I urge you to accept and confess Him now.

S E R M O N   X I

Stir Up the Gift of God

S E R M O N   X I

Stir Up the Gift of God

~~~~~~

> *Wherefore I put thee in remem-*
> *brance that thou stir up the gift of*
> *God, which is in thee.*
>
> II TIMOTHY 1:6

Paul was an old man when he thus wrote to the
young man Timothy. One of the sublimest things about
Paul's many-sided life was his interest in youth. More than
any other author in the New Testament, Paul manifested an
abiding interest in young people. This interest was evidenced
in his two letters to Timothy, the young preacher. The young
man appears not only frail in body, but timid and shrinking
in habit and character and life, and Paul summoned him—
he challenged him—in these words of the text: "I put thee in
remembrance that thou stir up the gift of God, which is in
thee." Paul's interest in youth is to the last degree suggestive
for us.

Somebody asked Sir Humphrey Davy, that wonderful dis-
coverer, what he regarded as his greatest discovery, and without a moment's hesitation he said: "My greatest discovery is
the discovery of Michael Faraday"—the discovery of a man
and the putting of his spirit in that man, so that Michael
Faraday, the younger, could take up the work of the older,
when the older had left the stage of action. And Agassiz,
another notable scientist, was once asked what he regarded
as the greatest work of his life, and he instantly replied: "My
greatest work of life, if anything I have done can be called
great, has been the training of two men to live like life ought
to be lived." And when Jesus, the great Head over His

church and the guide for all mankind, the Light of the World, came to do His blessed work, He took twelve men aside, and for three years he drilled them and taught them and impregnated them with His ideas, His ideals. Jesus pursued the best method of all, the one abiding method. He chose a few and put His truth, His ideas, His ideals, His spirit, into them. Shortly before leaving them He said: I have chosen you. I now lay my mantle on your shoulders. You must go out and take the world. I have told you about it. Go now and do it." That was His method. And it was Paul's method, too. Jesus never put emphasis on the crowd. He always put emphasis on the individual. Save the individual and society is saved. Lose the indivdual and society is lost. Christ is differentiated from every other teacher, in that He looks after the one person, and puts His spirit, His power, His call, in the heart of one person.

And now the Apostle Paul takes this young preacher, gifted Timothy, and says: "I put thee in remembrance that thou stir up the gift of God which is in thee"; or, as the original has it, "That thou dost kindle into the highest flame that you can make burn every power wherewith God hath endowed you." That is what he says.

Now, what is this gift of God in us, each one of us? What is this gift of God in each of us, you and me? There is a variety of gifts. No two people have the same gifts. Some men have five talents, and some have two, and some have one. There is diversity everywhere among mankind, just as there is diversity everywhere in the forest about us, but every person is given of God some gift, and God says: "I want that gift enlivened, awakened, kindled, brought to the highest, for Myself."

Now, what is the gift that is in us which needs enlivening, needs inflaming, needs kindling, needs stirring up? I may name several, which will not be a complete inventory of all the gifts at all, but they will be indicative, they will be suggestive, and you will think of others. Indeed, at the prayer meeting Wednesday night I suppose we named fifteen or twenty. Let us name half a dozen this evening, with a passing word in each case.

First of all, there is the *gift of speech*. Oh, what a regal gift is the gift of speech! A horse, however proud and sprightly, and the great lion, however courageous yonder in the forest, may be brought here to this platform for us to behold; and, though they may be strikingly attractive to us all, they do not have the regal gift that I am now putting forth, the gift of speech. There is an impassable gulf between the highest animal of the animal creation about us and the lowest man that walks the earth this night, and that gulf may be indicated by man's regal, noble gift of speech. Now, this gift of speech ought not to be perverted; it ought not to be prostituted; it ought not to be debauched; it ought not to be wasted. Jesus comes to us saying: "I want every friend I have to be a talker, to be a witness, to be a champion, to be a pleader for Me—every friend I have; not simply the preacher, not simply the prophet, but I want every friend I have to stir up the gift of speech and talk for Me everywhere. Talk for Me everywhere." That is Jesus' great call to us.

I raise the question for the young person hearing me to-night, and the older one as well: "Are you using the gift of speech for Christ?" You remember that great convict, condemned to death in Britain awhile ago for one of the most flagrant crimes in British history. He utterly refused to let any Christian talk to him after his condemnation to be executed on a certain day. He utterly put away, scorned every approach that any Christian made to talk to him about Christ. By and by the next to the last day came, and somehow a preacher got inside his cell and was talking with the man before he realized that a preacher had come. The man was utterly indifferent, utterly irresponsive to the preacher's approach, and presently the preacher said: "Don't you know that you will die tomorrow?" "I know it quite well. I know it better than you do," said the man. "I am quite conscious

157

of such fact." And then the preacher said: "If you die, not being a friend to Christ, not repenting of your sins, not trusting yourself to Jesus, who came and died for sinners— if you die tomorrow and go into the next world without making peace with Him—you will have lost the soul and happiness and peace forever?" The convict turned upon the preacher and glowered upon him like some wild beast in his lair, and said to him: "Why, man, I do not believe a word of it. Nobody ever told me that before. I do not believe a word of it. If that were true, somebody long ago would have stopped me and told me that I had everything at stake. Somebody would have reminded me of that ere this." And then he turned to the preacher and said: "If I believed with you what you have just said, I would go out and tell that to every man in Great Britain, if I had to crawl on my knees to get it told." Now, when we think of the power of the human tongue to turn one whose feet are in the stocks of death away from such stocks into the way of life—to do it by speech—how important that such gift be stirred up, the gift of speech!

And young people can reach young people better than anybody else in the world can reach them. Many are the times that I speak to the students here and there in the schools and colleges and, oh, it is wonderful to see a young fellow go after his chum, his comrade, his pal! It is wonderful to see a young girl go out after her friend, seeking by personal speech to point out to her the heavenward road. Again and again I have seen boys in their teens with their serious faces going out after their chums and comrades, and girls of the same age doing likewise, and the victories are overwhelming and glorious. Young people, while you are yet young people, I summon you—I beseech you—in Christ's name, use your gift of speech now to get people to Christ, while you are young.

What other gift is to be stirred up? There is _the gift of writing._ How few people make enough of the gift of writing? Somebody has well said that if any boy or girl would take pains to write carefully fifty words a day on some high subject

—every day fifty words—after a while you would be astonished at your own vocabulary and at your own splendid discipline that would come from such practice. Everyone who can write things that will help ought to write; and it ought to be a habit with young people, and older ones as well, to write a letter, useful and vital and sympathetic and religious, every time that the way is open. Delicately and courteously and thoughtfully and prayerfully, such letter ought to be written.

I am thinking now of one of our distinguished citizens, who died a little while ago in this city unexpectedly. I was shown by his family a little box that he kept, a little private box, in which he kept certain little trinkets, that he never allowed anybody to see. Nobody carried the key but himself. But the family showed me that box after we had finished the funeral. A day or two had passed, and they showed me that box after they had opened it. There was a little lock of hair. The great business man had kept it as a memento of the little baby girl who went away long, long ago. And there was this, and there was that, and there was the other. And then I found a letter in that box, written by one of our men in this church, to that big business man, pouring out his soul to that man, begging him to come to Christ. It was a simple, straight-forward, manly, honest, Christian letter. He said: "I beg pardon if you think it is a presumption. If you think it is an impertinence I beg pardon. I am writing out of the sheerest unselfishness. I am writing because I think of you often, and I covet your great life for Christ." And that letter was so prized by the man who received it that he put it away in that box and never spoke of it to a soul. His wife and children said: "We never knew of it until we opened the box and found it." I went and asked the man who wrote it: "Did you ever get any reply?" He said: "None at all. I wonder if he treated it as an impertinence." I said: "No. He put it away in a little box, where he kept his treasures. He prized it beyond words."

Every young Christian who hears me ought to form the habit of writing courteous, kindly and deferential letters, to people about you who need to be won to the side and service of Christ. Of course, every such letter should be written with prayer for divine guidance. What if these hundreds and hundreds of Christians listening to me tonight should each one write the right kind of a letter to somebody at least once a week! Think how many you would have written in one year, and think how wide-spread would be the lines of light and power that would attend such letters. Stir up that gift.

What other gift have you to stir up? Everyone of us has the *gift of influence*, and what a great gift it is! No man ought ever to harm his influence. That is the reason I do not do certain things. I could go to certain places and do certain things, maybe, without being hurt myself; but if this would harm somebody else, that ends it. "If eating meat causes my brother to stumble, I will eat no meat while the world standeth," said Paul. We have our influence. No one lives to himself, nor does anyone die to himself. Now, we are to take our influence and we are to bring all that influence over to Jesus, and on His side put it, and we are to make our influence to the last degree count — not for the minimum of good, but the maximum of good; not how little we can be and do for the right, but how great our service, how large our helpfulness — that is to be our program.

What other gift are we to stirr up? We are to stir up the *gift of experience* which we already have. Every person has some personal experience which he needs to pass on to somebody else. There is no teacher so effective as personal experience. If a person comes to you saying, "I want to tell you something that I have tried, and tested and proven to be true and helpful," your ears are at once alert to hear his testimony. When somebody comes in touch with your life and to that one you say, "I want to tell you about Christianity in my case, about counsel that I get from God, about divine light and leading that I have from God," you will pass on a power and an experience to somebody else which may prove to be an abiding blessing to that one.

I think I have told some of you that, two weeks after I became a Christian I was unspeakably cast down in spirit. I was in the deepest Slough of Despond. I wondered if I had not utterly missed the right road and made shipwreck of my soul. But there was an older Christian — a young man, but a few years older than myself (I was barely grown) who seemed intuitively to know that I was in trouble. He said to me one Sunday morning: "I will be over at your house this afternoon, if you are free, for I want to take a walk, and have a talk." He came, and we went in the great woods, in the presence of the majestic trees, and he said: "I have wondered how you are getting along. You are just two weeks old as a Christian. I saw you when you confessed Christ publicly and took your place in the church. I have been ten years on the road," he said, "and I thought I would tell you of certain ups and downs I have had, of certain horrible doubts." He told me of his experiences and, in so doing, he described my case far better than I could have told him. When we came back from that walk in the woods I had passed an epoch in my life, the glory of which two hours has stayed with me ever since.

Pass on your experience to somebody else. Let the older Christian brace the younger Christian. Let the older Christian give counsel, give good cheer, give inspiration, ask questions, proffer a brother's help. Let the older brother help the younger brother. Let the older sister come with words kindly and helpful to the little sister; and thus we can, in a mighty way, stir up the gift of experience by passing it on to others.

What other gift shall we stir up? There is the great *gift of prayer.* We talk about waste. My dear friends, was there ever another waste so tragical as the waste that comes from not praying? The Bible tells us: "Ye have not because ye

161

ask not." Was there ever another tragedy comparable to the tragedy which comes from not praying? The greatest forces about us are latent forces. Electricity, playing there in those clouds, the world did not know about and could not harness until just a little while ago. Oh, that the world might learn the marvelous meaning of stirring up the gift of prayer! Do you pray for people? For whom do you pray? Do you pray for that tempted young Christian and that untaught, inexperienced young Christian? Do you pray for that man down in the depths of temptation? Do you pray that God will open His hand and pour upon the community and on the world His own great blessings of grace and healing and health? How much do you pray? Stir up the gift of prayer. And that gift of secret prayer, magnify it to the last degree.

There is the *gift of business ability.* This gift is possessed by many men. They have a talent for making money, much money, and they can use that money to make the flowers grow on ten thousand wildernesses. Do you know the story of the great candy maker, Mr. Huyler? It is one of the most thrilling stories in the whole history of the triumph of the Christian religion. If you will see how that famed candy manufacturer takes his great business sense and takes his vast income, and scatters it like the leaves of Vallombrosa, everywhere, to better the world, you will wonder, as I wondered when I recently read his life story: "Is there a preacher between the oceans doing as much as that one man?" Consider Mr. Colgate. Recently I spoke at the university which bears his name, there in the state of New York. As you know he was a great soap manufacturer. He came with his habits of simplicity and frugality and economy and sincerity, and old-fashioned honesty, and family prayer morning and night. He built up a great fortune which he used well and wisely. He saved a struggling college, and made it one of America's best. He reinforced many other worthy causes and institutions throughout the nation. He stirred up the gift that was within him. Yes, some men can make money and by its proper use give it ten thousand tongues for good.

The gifts of God within you may be anyone of a multitude of talents or special abilities. Whatever the gift, it should be stirred up, kindled into a flame, that it may burn for the glory of God and the blessing of the world.

The question naturally arises as to *how* we shall stir up the gift of God within us. First, we should take account of the gifts we now have. Every person here should list his assets. And what are your assets? Well, to start with, you are a human being. Oh, what a wonderful thing that God did not make you a horse, or a tree, or a blade of grass. You are a physical, mental, moral, social, and spiritual being. A sane mind in a sound body is a blessed asset. Essentially you are a soul that shall live when those stars and that moon and that great sun are laid aside forever. You will live on. By your moral choices and your social behavior you can demonstrate what it means to be a child of God. What marvelous assets! Take account of them. See what you can best do. See what you can do here and there and yonder. How much can you talk, and how much can you write, and how much can you do this, and do that, and do the other? Discover, cultivate, train, develop your assets. That means work and more work: that means practice and more practice; that means training, training, training. People do not accidentally make great successses of their lives. I dare say that there never lived a more indefatigable toiler than Thomas A. Edison, that great wizard in the realm of invention. And that man Paderewski is not simply some freak with long hair making music for the world. He, too, is a prodigious toiler. Throughout the long years he has never let up on his daily practice at his piano. That is one reason why he became the master musician that he is. The men who succeed are men who take their assets of body and hand and brain and spirit and all, and develop them, call them out, train them, discipline them, bring them to their highest and to their best.

163

Again, we must stir up our gifts by use. Gifts will rust if they be not used. There are good, Christian men here tonight listening to me who never led a public prayer in a church house in their lives. If they had only practiced and done their best, beginning stammeringly, as I did, and able to pray only one sentence, as I was able in my first prayer — only one, for my tongue did cleave to the roof of my mouth, and I could not think of another word to say — if those men here who love Christ had prayed in public and done the best they could, now they could pray in public and the hearts of the hearers would be enraptured with symphonies from God's world above as they heard these men pray. If only they had developed that gift! And so with all the rest. Are you using your gifts? Or are you letting them rust? Are you letting them go to waste? Any gift you have, use it to the best and to the highest for Christ. Stir it up that way. Use means increase. Disuse means decrease. Use means enlargement. Non-use means loss. That is true universally. Take any gift on earth and do the best you can with it, and God will add His divine power, and the best will come to pass.

Pray God to help you. O young people, pray unto God about your powers. Ask God: "Where is the niche, Father, that Thou wouldst have me fill? Ought I to be a merchant? Very well. A lawyer? Very well. A teacher? Well and good. A banker? All right. A farmer, a ranchman? What is the niche, Lord, that I should fill? Show it to me and let me get ready for it, with learning, with information, with right habits of preparedness, with preparation. Let me be ready for that niche." If you pray like that you will get divine light and leading.

Why should we stir up these gifts? First of all, just because of plain duty. Do you know how that word "duty" used to be spelled? We spell it now d-u-t-y, but of old it was spelled d-u-e-t-y, and that is what the word always means: "something due," yes, "something due." We owe it to God. It is due from us to God, not to be drones, not to be dullards, not to be sluggards, not to be loafers. We owe it to God to do our best. I am warned every week about burning up my life, but I would rather die at fifty, living at the maximum, than to live to be one hundred and fifty years and rust clear on to the last. We owe it to Christ, and we owe it to ourselves, and we owe it to Christ's church — which needs an impassioned and trained and educated people — to do our best at preparation, at training and at service to the world about us.

Why stir up the gift within? Because consistency demands it. Shall a Christian be a dullard, sluggard, a loafer, and incompetent person? After Jesus poured out the last drop of His blood on yonder cross for you, shall you barely give the old scraps and begrudge them to your Lord, who claims you and owns you by the rights of creation, and redemption, and preservation?

Our gifts should be stirred up because of our incomparable opportunity now. John C. Calhoun, that great United States senator, began his greatest speech in the United States Senate by saying: "Fellow-senators: I begin my speech by asking you to lift up your minds to the level of the conditions that now confront our country." O my young Christians, and young people not Christians, and older ones as well, would God that one time we might lift up our minds to the level of the conditions that now confront the world! Desperately the world needs now the message and the ministry of the churches of our Lord Jesus Christ. But alas! So many of His churches are terribly handicapped by the lack of trained and efficient leadership and by the lack of intelligent and whole-hearted service by the membership. We should be challenged by the greatness of the opportunities which now confront us. Big ideas make big people. Little ideas make little people. It could not be otherwise. Let a man dwell on petty ideas and presently he will be talking pettily and his mouth will have a petty turn to it. We are transformed, to a remarkable degree, by our ideas and our ideals. The ideas and ideals of Jesus can change us from narrow provincials into world-citizens. A man in close fellowship with Jesus cannot remain little. He cannot be petty and nasty and mean in his spirit. Big ideas make great people.

Jesus comes with His world ideals. The greatest picture I have ever seen of Jesus is one in which He stands holding the world in His hand. That is what He wants us to see now. No more provincialism at all! We are world-citizens. The citizens living in Dallas, these young men and women before me tonight, are world-citizens. The World Wars have made us such, and we are bound up vitally and inexplicably tonight with England and with France and with the rest of the world. We are world-citizens. World-citizenship calls for training. World-citizenship calls for knowledge. World-citizenship calls for preparation. World-citizenship calls for study of the Bible. World-citizenship calls for study of the meaning of Christ's church. World-citizenship calls for efficiency. Oh, by the world-citizenship that has been thrust upon us in the strange providence of God, let us stir up our gifts to their highest and noblest possibilities.

And then, in a little while, we shall lay the business all down. In a little while we shall put the politics aside. In a little while the teacher will come back from the school-room for the last time. In a little while the editor will have written his last editorial, the doctor will have made his last call, the lawyer will have addressed his last court and jury. In a little while time will be at an end for us. Oh, by the speedy approach of that time out there, let us live while we live to the highest glory of God.

> We are living, we are dwelling,
>   In a grand and awful time;
> In an age on ages telling,
>   To be living is sublime.

My men and women, and especially my young people — the apple of mine eye, the joy of my soul — give your best now in training and in service for Jesus, your Lord. Let us pray.

SERMON XII

Trumpeting the Gospel

Trumpeting the Gospel*

~~~~~~

> *From you sounded out the Word of the Lord, not only in Macedonia and Achaia, but also in every place your faith to God-ward is spread abroad; so that we need not speak anything.*   I THESSALONIANS 1:8

PAUL is here paying a most remarkable compliment to the church at Thessalonica. We shall search in vain in all the Scriptures for a more delicate and beautiful, and yet more worthy compliment than this paid by Paul to that old-time church. Paul's compliments were worth having. He was no fulsome flatterer. He was discriminating and just, sincere and true; and therefore the more beautiful and significant stands out this compliment that Paul paid that church. "You are a dynamic force for the Gospel," said Paul; "you have made, and are making, an impression for it so wonderful that I do not need to say one word." Did you ever note a more desirable compliment?

Some time before this Paul had gone from Philippi, where he had been assaulted, maltreated, beaten, into this pagan city of Thessalonica. When he opened his lips to speak the wonderful words of life, there was a remarkable response right in the heart of that heathen capital. Men who served idols, men steeped in the lust of idolatry and in the basest forms of vice that enshrouded that city, heard this man tell about One who came from the Father's house to reveal the Father's love, and who gave Himself to break the shackles

---

*Reprinted by permission of Fleming H. Revell Co., New York, N. Y., from *We Would See Jesus.*

from men who would be disenthralled, and who would walk in the sunlight of truth and righteousness. And they believed that message, and from that hour they voiced it with their noble living. From that hour their lives were fundamentally changed.

You have noted, haven't you, what an eye Paul had for strategic places? He was a seer. He had the forecast of the first statesman of the world. He knew that what was done in a city was a thing not done in a corner, but everybody would hear about it and know about it, and feel it, according to whether it should be good or bad. He knew that, and he put that great heart and hand and brain of his on the city. As goes the city so shall go the country and the whole land. The city is the nerve-center and the storm-center of civilization and of Christianity. If these cities are not saved, Christianity is lost and all is lost. If these cities are saved the whole land shall be vocal with the songs of heaven, Paul knew that, and that statesman-like eye of his swept those cities of Europe and Asia, and his heart coveted those centers, those strongholds for God.

Let everybody keep his eye on the city. That little remote village yonder, far in the country place, away from the noise and confusion of the city, is vitally interested in what we do here in the city, and we must not forget this, nor must they. A road leads from that little village, or from that remote country schoolhouse to the city; and not only does the road lead here, but the boy out there is coming here, and we shall contaminate him and damn him, or we shall disenthrall him and add to his strength and nobleness, and send him back a joy to the old folks who sent him away with so much concern. The little remote country community is vitally interested in the city, interested in its laws, interested in it in every respect. There is no drawing a line and saying, "The city shall stay on this side." It isn't going to do it. "And the country shall stay on that side." It isn't going to do it.

We are neighbors, and ever becoming more so, mingling and intermingling. We are to plan our deeds of noblest strength right in the heart of the city. Paul did that in Thessalonica, and in the other cities of the time in which he lived, showing what an eye he had for strategic situations.

Did you notice this expressive word that Paul employed? We come upon it here for the first time, and I think the only time in the New Testament, in its description of the business of a church: "From you sounded out the word of life." The church is to be God's trumpet. "From you is trumpeted forth the word of life." From this trumpet the word of life is to be sounded forth. A church is God's agency supreme in the world through which His love is revealed and His grace made known. That is the business of a church, and here it is strikingly set forth.

Let us look at two or three vital truths that are enwrapped in this compliment Paul pays to the church at Thessalonica.

And, first, he tells us the kind of men that sounded out the word of life. The context gives us the description of such men. They were men who possessed the fundamental virtues of the Christian life, the cardinal virtues, the vital virtues — three of them. "Remembering," said Paul, "without ceasing, your work of faith, your labor of love, and your patience of hope in our Lord Jesus Christ." These are the fundamental Christian virtues, and these Christians in Thessalonica possessed them. "Your work of faith, your labor of love, your patience of hope." What a trio that, and how fond Paul was of such trios! In concluding that incomparable chapter on Love, the thirteenth chapter of First Corinthians, Paul said: "And now abideth faith, hope, love, these three; but the greatest of these is love." The abiding virtues, the cardinal virtues, the fundamental virtues in a Christian life, were possessed by these Thessalonian Christians, who sounded forth the word of life.

171

And Paul further said: "You were possessed by these virtues; you did not receive the Gospel in word only, but also in power, and in the Holy Ghost, and in much assurance." "That is to say," said Paul, "you were absorbed by these great matters; you took your religion seriously; you accounted it the first thing in the world to be true followers of God, to be faithful imitators of Christ." And still further, said Paul, "You held constant, you were invariable in the midst of sorest trials." Go read again in the book of the Acts, and see how those early Christians in Thessalonica were assaulted by the mob, how their blood flowed down their backs from the scourgings laid on them by cruel persecutors. Mark how they were hunted like the wild beasts on the mountains, how they watched and yet as they watched, mark how they sang their songs of praise and voiced their hymns of obedience to Jesus! Paul said to those Christians: "You were constant in the midst of sorest trials; you did not recant when the battle became fierce; you did not flee, coward-like, when the stress of the storm was on you; you were true." Oh, what a tribute was that for Paul to pay a little group of Christians, that they were constant, that they were invariable, that they obeyed without wavering! What tribute was that!

I have had occasion to say it before, but I would say it again and again — I care less and less for what you are pleased to term your brilliant man. I care more and more for your dependable man — the man true in every storm, the man who, when people discuss him in their little circles and cliques and caucuses, must say: "You may put that man down as on the side of right though the heavens fall." Your dependable man, your man who is not a weather-vane, your man who does not try to ride two horses at the same time going in opposite directions, he is the salt of the earth, the life-blood of civilization. William Pitt made correct answer when one asked him one day: "Mr. Pitt, what would you pronounce the first qualification for a prime minister of Great

Britain?" And he said: "The first qualification is patience." Said the questioner: "What would you pronounce the second qualification for a prime minister of Great Britain?" And Pitt replied: "The second qualification is patience." "Well, then," said the questioner, "what would you pronounce the third qualification?" And he said: "The third is patience." Wasn't it wisely said? We need patience to hold on, patience to plod, patience to persevere, patience to keep at our work without wavering or fainting. "Be thou faithful unto death"—not until death—that isn't what it says, that isn't what it means. "Be thou faithful unto death"—that is, die before being unfaithful. Any man ought to prefer any hour to die than to play the ignominious traitor and be unfaithful to the right thing. "Be thou faithful unto death" — die before being unfaithful — "and" — note the great promise — "I will give thee the crown of life." Now such were the men to whom Paul paid this incomparable compliment.

Notice here also the means that they employed for sounding out this word of God, this Gospel of life. The context explains that fully for us. First of all, the chief means for sounding out this conquering Gospel was that such Gospel produced in debauched lives the most marvelous transformations. There is nothing else in the world so moving, so startling, as for a man to be soundly converted by the Gopsel of God. These men of Thessalonica were converted all over, they were fundamentally changed. They had long served idols but when Paul's gospel came in, breaking those idols into dust, presenting Jesus, the Way, the Truth, and the Life, the Emancipator of sin-driven men, the Life-Bringer, the Hope-Giver — when they heard that, they turned away from their idols to serve the living and true God, and to wait for His Son from heaven, whom He raised from the dead, even Jesus, who delivered us from the wrath to come. There is nothing so wonderful as a true conversion, as for a man to be genuinely saved. We are hearing a great deal these days about all manner of prescriptions for advancing Christianity. They are telling us much, these days, about "socializing Christianity." I am shy of much of that kind of talk. The greatest thing in the world is for the individual man to be saved by the gospel, for such man to have a divine power come into his life and turn him to God. That is the greatest thing in the world. The best advertisement for this gospel which we love is a saved man, living his religion. That is the supreme advertisement. Paul said: "You men are my advertisement; you are such a good advertisement I do not need to speak anything." Did you ever hear a more wonderful compliment than that? Oh, this is to be our glory, our predominant passion, to see men saved, to see men converted divinely by this glorious gospel, transformed, changed, saved!

I have told you before, I think, of the most remarkable conversion I ever saw. Will you bear with me while I tell you again about it? The occasion was several years ago, in a great outdoor Texas meeting. Conditions religiously were dreadfully hard and bad where such meeting was held. I think I never knew them worse. Men with white locks about their ears were lost, and even their grandchildren followed in forbidden and ruinous paths; and the few people of God in the community were down and beaten and defeated, it seemed. One of the causes for such conditions was that a group of men had had a series of little, pesky, religious debates, and the result was that conditions were hard and harsh and bad on every side.

All these things were recounted in the preacher's ears, as he began the meetings. I shall never forget the repeated story of the people there concerning one of their citizens, a man known for a radius of hundreds of miles. I could speak his name, but will not. He would not forbid it, for I could speak it to God's praise. They told me much about this same "Big Jim." They said: "He will come to the meeting once this year; then he will curse you and the meeting out, and curse the churches, and then he will wait another year to come again. That is his style. You need not waste any preaching on him." They described him so that I could not mistake him — he was the largest man in all that section. One night I stood up to preach, and in came Big Jim. I shall never forget the emotions that then possessed me. Here was "the chief of sinners," so the people said. What could be done for him?

That night I preached, and God's Spirit moved upon the audience mightily, and men with their white locks and stooped shoulders were, like little children, that night turned to the Saviour. Grandfathers that night came, who had walked the wrong way for well-nigh their threescore years and ten. And their grandchildren also came. The Spirit of the Lord was upon us in marvelous fashion that night.

Yonder sat Big Jim like a granite shaft. And when that service was concluded, a little group of people stayed behind and talked with one another about the hour just past, as men are wont to talk over such an occasion. Ever and anon they would refer to Big Jim. They said: "He was here to-night, but he won't be back." One said, "I believe he will return; I never saw him look as he looked to-night." Another said, "No"; another said, "Yes." Presently, after I had left the tabernacle to find the cottage where I slept, as I went along through the quiet woods, I heard some one talking in the darkness of the night. I did not mean to be an eaves-dropper. There were two of them talking, oh, so earnestly. They were talking to God. This is what they were saying: "Mighty God, the people are saying that Big Jim is too much for Thee. Oh, break to pieces our unbelief, and let all this country know that God is Master of the situation, that He can save even the chief sinner here!" They said: "Master, we plead Thy promise to Thy disciples about two who may agree, and if agreeing concerning anything they should ask, Thou wilt hear. We agree that we want Big Jim saved for the glory of God, and to stop the mouths of gainsayers once and forever in all this section."

I quietly went my way, leaving them thus on their knees. They did not know that I had heard them, nor do I know who they were. The next day came and wore to evening, and again I stood up to preach, and in came Big Jim again. Yonder he sat at the rear of the tabernacle; and then I said, "Father, give me the word of life for this brother man."

I told the story of the prodigal son, that restless, wayward lad, who went away from home against the protest of love and wisdom's voice, and who went from bad to worse, until yonder he was in the swine fields eating of the husks wherewith he fed the swine. One day the prodigal became homesick and soul-sick and he said: "I have missed it all; my whole life's course is a grim sarcasm; I have missed it all. I can do better than this as a servant in my father's house; and worst of all, worst of all, I have sinned against my best friend, I have sinned against my father who loved me, and I have sinned against my father's God. I will go back and I will tell him all." You know the rest. You know how the father, whose heart ached because the boy was gone, looked one day and saw him coming, and while he was yet a great way off, that father ran to meet him and to fold that thing of rags and shame to his heart, while the boy wept and said: "Father, I did not come back to ask to be your boy, but to tell you that I have sinned against you and heaven, and that I am not worthy to be called your son, but ask only to have a servant's place." And the father said: "Kill the fatted calf for the boy returned; bring him the best robe; put on his finger the ring — emblem of love that never dies." That was what I preached. And then I said: "I bring you a gospel to which I have anchored my very soul; I am willing to die by it, and I am trying to live by it; I am going to meet God with it when I stand before Him in the judgment. I came one day and surrendered to that Saviour whom God the

Father sent. Is there a man here who will surrender to Him now?"

Big Jim started towards the preacher, and in a moment half a thousand men were seeing him and all these rose to their feet. Were they dreaming? Was it too good to be true? They were on their feet, looking, listening, sobbing. Down that long aisle came Big Jim, and when he reached me he caught my hand and said: "I put you on your sacred honor — will Jesus Christ save me if I give up to Him?" I said: "On my sacred honor, I answer that He will." And then he looked at me again while the men, who stood all about us now, were begging him to yield to Christ. He spoke again: "But you must remember that I am the worst man out of hell." I answered back: "My Saviour died for the worst man out of hell, and He is able to save him now." Once more he looked at me and said: "When would He save me if I were to surrender myself to Him right now?" I said: "On the authority of Jesus Christ, on which I have rested my soul for time and eternity, I declare that He will save you right now, and you yourself may be the judge, if you will fully surrender to Him now."

Then he turned that great, bronzed face, pitiful in its anguish, up towards the heavens, and gasped this prayer: "Lord Jesus, the worst man in the world gives up to you right now!"

I cannot tell you all the rest. I don't know that the angels could tell it all. But God unloosed his tongue, and Big Jim witnessed for Jesus then and there as I never heard Him witnessed for before nor since. Old, grizzled men came and kissed Big Jim; and old women came and kissed him; and little children kissed him, for the chief of sinners was saved. And then the word went to and fro as fast as the winds could carry it that God was in the midst of the people forgiving sin.

177

Gentlemen, one such apologetic as that for Christianity sounds out the gospel word both far and near as can nothing else in all the earth. We will stay by the simple, old-fashioned, supreme vocation of Christ's church, and that is to win men to God. That is the biggest thing in all the world. And when that is done, light will spread and darkness will flee, and righteousness will follow. That was the way the gospel of old was made victorious. Men were converted to God and others soon heard the glad news, and themselves were led to ask the way of life.

Then, again, these Thessalonians, by their lives, attested their profession. Their profession was vindicated by their lives. Paul said: "Your life has been so glorious, you have been such an inspiration, such a blessing, such an example to all the people throughout all Greece, north and south, that I do not even need to say a word in defense of the gospel. You are the gospel embodied, you are the gospel incarnated in lives, you are the gospel lighting up a house that was once inhabited by black, evil things, and now shines to the praise of God." Their lives attested their profession.

Here is the best argument for Christianity: The right kind of a Christian — mark you the right kind of a Christian. He is the one unanswerable, invulnerable argument for Christianity in this world — the right kind of a Christian. These men said, wherever they went throughout Greece, north and south, all through Macedonia, all through Achaia, wherever they went, they said: "We were debauched, we were bad, we were enslaved, we were handicapped by sin, we were depraved. We accepted Christ, and He changed our natures; we are now new men." And their lives said it much louder than anything their lips could say. That is the power of the gospel.

Oh, my fellow Christians, that is its irresistible power! You can feel some men, the Christian element in them is so strong. That was the glory of Phillips Brooks. You could not analyze his preaching, but you could feel him. That was the glory of Robert E. Lee, that matchless man of Southern history. That was the glory of William Pitt, Prime Minister of Great Britain. That was the glory of Washington, Father of His Country. That is the glory of many a little, modest man, and many a little, shrinking woman, whose life is radiant with the sunlight of sincerity, and with a glorious enduement of God's goodness and truth and grace. These men of old thus lived their religion.

There was another thing that was conquering in their Christian character, and that was their faith was as clear as the sunlight, and as enduring as a granite mountain. Their faith — what a vital word is that! What a vital word that is for these times, with all the theological vagaries we have about us, and all the fads and fancies, the cults and innovations! Their faith was as clear as the sunlight, as unshakable as Gibraltar. These men knew what they believed, and why; and they were able to give to every man they met an answer for that marvelous hope that illumined their way, and transformed their lives.

I would summon you to-day, my fellow Christians, to be clear in your faith. Know what you believe concerning the things of religion, and why. The man who speaks with the accent of sincerity and definiteness is the man of power. Remember the apostle's question: "If the trumpet give an uncertain sound" — (and remember we are trumpets for Christ) — "if the trumpet give an uncertain sound, who shall prepare himself to the battle?" Your testimony for God is to be clear and unhesitating and certain. Alas! that some Christians in their faith are like Reuben of old, unstable as water, and like him, too, it may be said of each of them: "Thou shalt not excel." Be clear in your faith. Don't be religious mugwumps. Jesus was the very Prince of dogmatists, and His apostles after Him were to the last degree dogmatic in their faith. Listen to Peter: "Neither is there salvation in any other; for there is none other name under heaven

given among men, whereby we must be saved." That is dogmatic. Listen to John, that disciple of love and gentleness:
"Who is the liar, but he that denieth that Jesus is the Christ?
This is the anti-Christ, even he that denieth the Father and
the Son." Listen to Paul: "But though we, or an angel from
heaven, preach any other gospel unto you than that we have
preached unto you, let him be accursed." And to increase
the emphasis, he repeats it in the next verse. Oh, my fellow
Christians, on this tremendous matter of religous faith we
want to be as clear as the sunlight, and as unshakable as the
everlasting hills. " 'Tis conviction that convinces."

Take Karl Marx. He was the most dogmatic and pro-
nounced personality that Germany has produced in a hundred
years — that noted Socialist leader. Mighty passions and con-
victions and beliefs surged in his life, and he put the stamp
of his forceful personality throughout all Germany and
Europe, and the world. Certainly you do not agree and I
do not agree with many of his teachings; but when a man
with the passion and the conviction and the personality and
the power of Karl Marx goes across the world, men feel
him. There are numberless fires burning in human hearts
to-day because Karl Marx believed something. The world is
studying this hour the teachings of Socialism, because Karl
Marx believed something.

Take the Roman Catholic Church. She has two special
dogmas, which, both in season and out of season, she pro-
claims: The dogma of the church, and the dogma of the
mass. We cannot in the least degree accept her teachings
concerning the church and concerning the mass; and yet
that great body concerning which I would not willingly say
one improper or unjust word — that great body goes through
the earth proclaiming that the church should be supreme in
the regulation of all human conduct, in the home, in society,
in things political, everywhere. You stand amazed as do I,
that such dogma should have advocates. And you are the

more amazed at their other dogma that simple bread and wine are actually changed into the very flesh and blood of Jesus, their doctrine of transubstantiation, after the blessing of such bread and wine, by the proper ecclesiastic. And yet that mighty ecclesiasticism, through the centuries, has boldly taught these two dogmas, and has put the impress of such teachings in every land beneath the stars. They believe something — that explains it. I honor them, while utterly differing from them, for persisting evermore in urging those amazing dogmas, because they believe them.

And in the other days, when Martin Luther, that immortal Protestant, who before was a Catholic priest, came to believe the God-honoring doctrine that men are not justified by human works, nor by human righteousness of any sort, but that they are justified by faith in Jesus Christ, Luther went out and proclaimed the doctrine of justification by faith in such a way that he wrested Germany from the hands of the Pope, and thrilled the world with his mighty pronouncement of Protestantism. He believed something, and he avowed it. When he had determined to go to the Diet of Worms, and men tried to keep him from going because he would go in the face of probable death, together with every threatened punishment, he answered them back: "If there were as many devils as there are tiles on every roof in Wurtemberg, I can but go and say what my soul knows to be true." He believed something.

My fellow men, let us have a faith that does not change with every change of the moon. John Knox put his marvelous personality on Scotland and on every other land beneath the sun because he believed something. He rescued Scotland from the grip of unbelief because he believed something. And John Knox's daughter, Jane Welch, when they offered her her husband's freedom if he would recant, answered like this: "I would sooner have my husband's severed head brought me in a charger than for him to deny the things he has taught and believed." Oh, for a generation of great believers!

But there was another all important thing about these early Christians. They attested their faith by their deeds. They proved their religion by their works. They vindicated their hope by their deeds. That is the apologetic that we must have — just that. All my time could be spent on that one simple point. But I leave it after referring to just one incident in the life of David Brainerd. That noble missionary to the Indians, when he became so old and weak and crippled with rheumatism that it seemed there was nothing else that he could do but wait there in his little hut and die, was found one day kneeling on the floor, too feeble to sit in his chair, teaching a little Indian girl her A B C's. And men said: "What! Has it come to this? The great David Brainerd down on the floor teaching a little Indian girl her A B C's!" And he said: "Happy if with my latest breath I may be permitted even to teach a little Indian girl her A B C's."

You will make the application, won't you of this old-time text? Every church, I remarked in the beginning, is to be a trumpet for Jesus Christ — to voice the word and love of Jesus Christ. My beloved people here of this flock, you will make the application. The church at Thessalonica was well situated to influence many people. How like your own! Thessalonica was a city of extensive commerce. How like your own city here! The roads were many that came to and went from Thessalonica. How like your own! And the blows struck for Jesus Christ yonder in Thessalonica sounded out throughout all the province of Macedonia. Even so, a light here properly given will send its rays both near and far. A testimony here properly given will go far beyond your own community. Like Paul, who was a patriot, as every man ought to be, you can say to-day: "I am a citizen of no mean city." And by reason of the position you have, you are called upon to sound out the word of life, of righteousness and of truth in every blessed and glorious way.

God has providentially thrust you into an exceedingly responsible place. Do not shrink from it. Oh, certainly there are times when you want to flee to the woods never to come back, but you can't. God has providentially thrust you into the gaze of the people, far and near, and you are called upon all the more to witness worthily for Jesus Christ. Here in Dallas are several of our denominational Boards. Here is your State Mission Board, doing the largest state mission work in all the world. Here also is your Woman's Work, in its official organization. Here also is your Young People's Board. Here is your denominational paper. Here is your great hospital. Then God has given us this noble church, with her thousands of members. What a host of people! And your fear sometimes is as mine, that this church will be a hospital of people not active, instead of a barrack of soldiers aggressive for God.

And then think of the army of strangers within our gates. I have often wondered if our ministry to the strangers is not broader than our ministry to our own homes and firesides; for scarcely a day passes that some stranger near or far does not write to give grateful testimony to the blessing brought him in worship with us here. By all these facts we are called upon to be the right kind of men and women. Then see our various church agencies of this one church. See the Sunday school, the supreme opportunity of the church. To save a boy is an incomparable bigger thing than to save a man. To save a girl is more important than to save a woman, for you save a life as well as a soul when you save a child. Here, too, are our organizations for our hosts of young people. Here also are the multitudes of women with their many and mighty forces. There is nothing more pitiful than for a woman saved through the blood of Christ to have her energies diverted into some little, narrow, shallow channel of selfishness, to gratify some small, passing impulse. Some time ago a cultured woman came to her pastor, not in Dallas, I am glad to remark, to say there was a Buddhist lecturer in the city, and to ask if the pastor would not let the Buddhist lecturer have the pulpit from which to exploit Buddhism. The pastor was amazed that a woman, given her position in this country, of happiness and honor — given such position by Jesus Christ — would wish her pastor to offer his pulpit for the exploitation of Buddhism, when a woman in Buddhist countries slavishly waits on her husband, is not regarded as worthy to eat at the same table with him, gets such crumbs only as he chooses to give, and is taught that she does not have any soul at all. What a tragedy it is when a woman, whose chief charm is her religion, is diverted from her church life into little, shallow, narrow channels of thought and activity. What a tragedy when her life is taken up with religious cults and fads and isms, and the deep, practical things of Christianity are forgotten.

I summon the Christian women who are here to-day, given their incomparable position by the blood of the Son of God — I summon them to give their best to Jesus Christ and to His church. And these men, these saved men, I summon them to give their best to Jesus and His church. My fellow men, if Jesus Christ loved the church enough to die for it, you and I surely ought to love it enough to live for it. There are two great organizations in the world that are absolutely invaluable, the home and the church. If you and I are to plant our labors in life where they will count for the most, then let us consecrate our best labors for the home and for the church. The home has been wretchedly neglected. I might mention a host of agencies at work for the welfare of children that would have been made unnecessary by the right kind of homes. The church also has been sadly neglected.

It is a day of organizations now. Sometimes I have wondered if some men could find enough space on their coats to put all the buttons of the various organizations to which they belong. I have not a word of railing to say against such organizations, but I would say, my fellow Christian men, that in these short lives that you and I are to live, we ought to link our lives with those organizations which will count the most, and with the organizations that are of most vital value to a needy world. Let us invest our lives, our love, our money, our service, not so that the fruits and influences therefrom shall be evanescent like some passing cloud of the morning, but so that they may abide through all the coming years. I summon you to give your best to Christ, your best to Christ today and always.

I have been with you many years. Oh, I know the stress and the travail of the preacher's life! I have gone to my room a thousand times and asked God if I might be released from it all; and then the instant the words escaped my lips I have hastened to say: "Nay, Lord, nay, only give me grace to be the preacher I ought to be!" Often I sing:

> Happy if with my latest breath,
> I may but speak Thy name;
> Preach Christ to all, and gasp in death,
> "Behold! Behold the Lamb!"

My grandfather was a preacher through the long, long years. In his last illness his affliction was such that he could not lie on his bed for one moment for many days. But people came to him for a region of forty or fifty miles, and there sitting in his chair, with his last expiring breath, he preached Christ Jesus, the world's one and only but sufficient Saviour. I should like to go like that to the last, witnessing for Jesus. O my fellow Christians, I summon you to give Christ your best of love, of service, of life. His is the most virile, the most masculine, the most heroic, the sublimest business on earth —

the making of His gospel victorious everywhere. Give Him your best, your best, forevermore.

O my fellow Christians of this church — a church dearer to me than my heart's blood, God knows — my fellow Christians of this church, I summon you anew to-day to give your best to Christ; to be done with all playing at your religion; to be done with all lukewarmness. I summon you to come with the rich, red blood of human sympathy for all mankind, for good and bad, for high and low, for rich and poor, and give your best to win this city and state and world to Jesus, so that you may hear that plaudit which it were worth worlds at last to hear, "Well done, thou good and faithful servant."

SERMON XIII

Are You Ready?

S E R M O N   X I I I

Are You Ready?

~~~~~~

I am ready.

ROMANS 1:15

FREQUENTLY in the writings of Paul we come across his statement: "I am ready." These three words may well be regarded as a kind of motto for his life, after he had surrendered to Christ.

Before his revolutionary experience on the road to Damascus, Paul had been a bitter opponent of Christ and all His followers. In his earlier years Paul was notoriously hostile to Jesus. He believed that Jesus was a fraud and he did his utmost to destroy one whom he regarded as a pretender. He frankly tells us that he thought he was doing God's service when he was persecuting Christians and making conditions as terrible as he could for all who professed to be followers of Christ.

There came a day, however, when he underwent a complete change in his attitude toward Christ and His followers. That day and that experience in the life of Paul marked one of the great turning points in the history of Christianity.

You will recall that Saul, afterwards known as Paul, was on his way to the city of Damascus in his furious campaign of persecution of Christians wherever he could find them. Suddenly, at the noon hour, he was struck down and blinded by a great light from heaven. As he lay there prostrate upon the ground he heard a voice saying: "Saul, Saul, why persecutest thou me?" And Saul answered: "Who art thou, Lord?" And the same voice replied: "I am Jesus of Nazareth, whom

189

thou persecutest." Promptly, Saul, trembling and astonished, said: "Lord, what wilt thou have me to do?"

That question of Saul's marked the beginning of the attitude which, for the rest of his life, we find summarized in his saying, "I am ready." I think the world has no record of a greater change, a more revolutionary or resultful right-about-face, than the conversion of Saul of Tarsus, who became Paul the Apostle to the Gentiles, the one whose motto was, "I am ready."

In striking contrast to Paul was an old Saxon king called Ethelred, who was never ready for any demand or duty. Not quite ready at any time for any call, so much so that his people characterized him on the pages of history as Ethelred the Unready. One may well believe that the old Saxon has had many successors, for wherever a great cause is promulgated, there is some Ethelred who says: "I am for it, you understand, but this is not the time, conditions are inopportune; you had better defer until a more propitious time. I am deeply in sympathy but this is not the time." Ethelred, the old Saxon king, undoubtedly has many successors. Now, Paul, in marked contrast, said from that meeting—that memorable destiny-determining meeting with Christ on the Damascus road—from that time Paul said. "I am ready."

I cite four occasions when Paul used these words. First he said, "I am ready for service, anywhere that God wishes, whatever it may be, wherever it may take me, whatever it may cost me, I am ready for service in the cause of Christ." Here in his letter to the Romans he said: "So as much as in me is, I am ready to preach the gospel to you that are at Rome also." Paul longed to go to Rome, the chief capital of the world at that time, strong with military strength, great with organization, powerful with equipment for its day.

Paul was not ashamed to preach the gospel in the seven-hilled city of Rome where Virgil sang, where great orators had discoursed to the delight of the people. He was ready to stand in Rome and preach the gospel, because, said he, "I am not ashamed of this gospel, for it is the power of God unto salvation to everyone that believeth." It is the gospel universal. It is for the Jew. It is for the Gentile. It is for the philosopher. It is for the dullard. It is for everybody—a gospel universal, adequate and all-sufficient. Concerning the gospel of Christ, Paul could say: "It is a tried gospel. It is a tested gospel. It is a corroborated gospel. I have passed it through the crucible of my own life. I am ready to live for it, and I am ready to die for it. It is the hope of mankind, and wherever anybody will listen to me, I am ready to talk about this gospel."

Paul had the right view of the divine, dynamic, transforming gospel of the Son of God. He believed that nothing else would suffice for a needy world.

Men need help above themselves. Men must have help which comes down from God out of heaven. Ethics will not suffice, important as that science of human behavior is in its proper place. Statesmanship is not sufficient. Secular education will not take care of our needs. The stain of sin is on every life. The bewildering, poisoning power of sin is in every life. Paul said: "I know a remedy. I know a physician. I know a helper adequate for the ills of men, and I am ready to go anywhere in the world, at any cost to myself, to preach this gospel to the world." This is the right attitude for every Christian.

I saw the other day where England asked one of her great men, "How soon can you be ready to go out for England in this great world struggle?" He had many irons in the fire, but he said: "I can be ready in twenty-four hours." I saw where a Moravian mission secretary said to a volunteer: "One of our men has fallen at the front. How soon can you go out to take his place?" The volunteer replied: "Just as soon as I get my boots back from the cobbler. He is mending them now, then I will be ready to go. I am ready." That is the

191

right spirit for God's people. "So as much as in me is, I am ready to go to Rome. I am ready to go anywhere. I am ready to go with the odds all against me, with difficulties and distresses graver than man or angel can describe awaiting me. I am ready to go anywhere that Christ wants me to go." That was Paul's spirit. Was there ever, in all the tides of time, another who quite matched him?

Paul said again, in writing to the church at Corinth, "I am ready to go and help you in the difficult situation that has come to your church." Read the story and you will find that the church had in it difficulties that shamed the church. There in the church of Corinth they had no pastor, and they had an upheaving and a distraught and terrible situation. Having learned of the unhappy conditions which had arisen in the Corinthian church which he had organized, Paul wrote a very frank letter in which he offered to visit them at Corinth. He indicated that he was ready to come and speak some plain words to them. He never ceased to have the pastor's heart toward all the churches he founded on his missionary tours. By letters and by return visits he sought to help all the churches, especially so when they were pastorless—as was the church at Corinth when he wrote, saying: "I am ready to come and help you out of this difficult situation."

How terrible it is that one wrong life can upset a whole group of lives! The Bible says: "One sinner destroyeth much good." It also says: "Jeroboam, the son of Nebat, made Israel to sin." One life can have an infection that can be passed on to the hurt of many lives. Let some portion of the body be infected and the whole body is imperiled. These infections may come in various ways. Sometimes they are doctrinal. Sometimes a person may steer away from the sound doctrine and he or she is on the toboggan from that very instant. The Bible says, "Hold fast the form of sound words." You cannot play fast and loose with the truth. If you begin that, presently the infection will spread, the hurt will go near and far in its corroding and enervating and injurious influence. When some prominent and forceful Christian and church member gets off the right track, the results may be tragically upsetting to the cause of Christ in a whole community.

Paul wrote to the church at Philippi, his best loved church, the church that was most considerate of him, that did more beautiful and thoughtful things for the grand old soldier of Christ than did any other church—and said: "I tell you again what I have told you before, I tell you now, even with weeping, some of you so walk as to become the enemies of the cross of Christ." They claimed to be Christ's friends, and to be marching under His banner; but, as Paul saw them, they were carrying the baggage of Satan and their lives were contrary to their profession.

The bad example and harmful influence of these enemies of the cross of Christ, there in Paul's beloved church at Philippi, made a very difficult situation for all concerned. Therefore, Paul says: "I am ready to come to help you in your church which is distraught by evil influences among yourselves. I am ready to help you. The duty may be difficult and disagreeable, but you must meet it; you must not be quiet: you must not be silent."

The sin of silence may be just as grievous as the sin of speech, the sin of omission just as grievous as the sin of commission. People are sometimes turned grievously aside by the sin of omission, to their hurt and the hurt of many others who sooner or later may be involved.

Paul was urging upon the Philippians just what, in another letter, he urged upon the Galatians when he said: "Brethren, if a man be overtaken in a fault, ye which are spiritual, restore such an one in the spirit of meekness; considering thyself, lest thou also be tempted. Bear ye one another's burdens, and so fulfil the law of Christ."

Here is a great field for recovering lives that are drifting. Christians are to recover, reclaim, win back, restore lives that are wrong in God's sight, in the church or out, reclaiming Christians who are adrift, or those who are not Christians at all. Reclaim them! Win them! Restore them and do it in the right spirit, the spirit of meekness, the spirit of compassion, the spirit of Christ. Paul volunteered to help the Phlippian Christians fulfil the law of Christ by bearing the burden imposed upon the church by its erring members.

And then he said another word: "I am ready to suffer for Christ's sake." Friends told him that if he went up to Jerusalem, he would be bound and imprisoned and scourged and beaten, and he said: "What mean ye to weep, and to break my heart? I am ready not only to be bound in Jerusalem, I am ready to die there for the name of the Lord Jesus Christ. I do not shun suffering. I am ready to do it. Bonds and imprisonment await me wherever I go; I have no complaint, I have chosen for the will of God to be expressed in my life, and if I can express it part of the time in jail, the jail is what I ask for. If I can express it part of the time by preaching to a great company on Mars' Hill, I will do that. I am ready to suffer for Christ." Oh, how wonderful was the spirit of this blessed apostle of Christ!

Paul preached throughout Asia Minor. Paul preached throughout Europe. Paul preached the gospel in world-famed Greece, poor, bludgeoned, bleeding Greece about which we read so often in our newspapers these days. His constant declaration was: "I am ready to preach the gospel anywhere. I am ready to go anywhere, and the whippings they will give me and the jails they will put me in, all that will not deter me. I am ready to suffer unto death for the name of Christ."

No cheap religion is going to win the world. The friends of Christ everywhere will have to live their religion more heroically and more sacrificially if the world is to be won for Christ. No cheap religion is going to win the world.

The early Christians overcame Satan. Do you remember how? The last book in the Bible tells us in one sentence: "They overcame him by the blood of the Lamb, and by the word of their testimony; and they loved not their lives unto death." No cheap religion will ever win the world. We must be ready to suffer for Christ!

But if you are going to suffer awhile for Christ's sake, you who are in this church or who are listening in radio-land, you must remember that you can glorify Christ in that suffering. As you lie upon your couch and turn your face to the wall when sleep is gone, and pray for the coming morning, you are to remember that there is some great, wide, gracious, far-seeing plan which God is weaving out of it all—a robe of blessedness better than the days of your strong health. Ready to suffer for Christ! Mind how you behave when suffering comes!

"Beloved," said the Apostle Peter, "think it not strange concerning the fiery trial which is to try you, as though some strange thing happened unto you, but rejoice, inasmuch as ye are partakers of Christ's suffering; that when His glory shall be revealed, ye may be glad also with exceeding joy." Paul expressed the same thought in Second Corinthians 4:17: "Our light affliction, which is but for a moment, worketh for us a far more exceeding and eternal weight of glory." Heaven itself will be deeper and richer because of the pain and the tears and the trials that we undergo down here on earth in the flesh.

Paul said: "I am ready to suffer anywhere that Christ wants me to suffer. I am ready. I am wholly abandoned to Him. If

I can do more by being in jail, then let me go to jail. If I can do more by being cuffed and beaten and scourged and maltreated, if by going through that I can best help the cause of Christ forward, then the will of God be done." That attitude is not just weak sentimentality, it is not perfumed poetry; it is Christ-like heroism, it is the very essence of the gospel, it is rugged strength suitable to make foundation stones for the kingdom of God.

In the fourth chapter of Second Timothy we come upon another splendid "I am ready" saying of Paul: "I am now ready to be offered, and the time of my departure is at hand. I have fought a good fight, I have finished my course, I have kept the faith. Henceforth there is laid up for me a crown of righteousness which the Lord, the righteous judge, shall give me at that day: and not to me only, but unto all them also that love His appearing."

From this grand old soldier of the faith each one of us should learn to say and mean it: "I am ready to go across the stream separating the now from eternity; and if the seas shall be storm-swept, I have a Pilot who will see me across. If the night be dark, I have one with me who is the Light of the world. If my strength shall fail, my God is my strength and my help and my portion for He has said: 'I will not leave you nor forsake you. You need not worry about how nor where nor when your departure will be. Just leave the time and the summons of it to me, and I will take care of it in the right time and in the right way.'" Oh, that every one of us may be able to leave all in God's hands!

I talked with a strong man a few hours ago, hard by the gateway of death. He said, "It looked like I was just getting ready to live, and now I have the sentence of death upon me." I said to him: "If you could talk to the great Saviour who died for us all, and He should say to you: 'You can do more now for me, by waiting a little while on this side of the flood in the right spirit and then crossing it without a sigh or a fear, you can do more for men than if you were a well, strong man,' what would you say?" He waited for awhile, then said with a sob, "I hope I could say, 'Thy will be done: Thy will be done. God's will be done.' I am ready to go when He wants me to go, and while I wait I want it to be for His glory."

Do you know how George Whitefield died? He preached as no other man in his day. The fields were filled with people to hear him. He was a mighty preacher. The people followed him and loved him. One day he preached in the afternoon and until late in the evening and the crowd followed him from the field to his home. He went upstairs to rest and as he climbed the stairs, he carried a candle in his hand to light his way. They could see him, and they pressed into the house and all around it and he preached until that candle burned down to its socket. Then he lay down upon his bed and was quickly gone. God took him. How glorious to go like that! Just to preach on until the last!

Paul was ready to preach the gospel of Christ. Paul was ready to serve anywhere and everywhere for Christ. Paul was ready to suffer for the sake of Christ. Paul was ready to die and pass on, to live with Christ forever. Because he was wholly dedicated and ever ready to do God's will, wherever it led and whatever it cost, Paul greatly influenced for good his own and all succeeding centuries.

Are you ready? Oh, my fellow Christians, are you ready to live and love and serve and sacrifice and suffer if need be, in order that Christ may be glorified and His cause be set forward by you? Are you ready and willing to do God's will, cost what it may, believing deep down in your heart that His will is ever wise and best? Are you ready for Christ to have His way with you, since His way is ever in harmony with the Father's will?

197

As for myself, I can truthfully say that long ago I settled it that Christ could have His way with me. God forbid that I should speak boastfully about a decision so vital and destiny-determining! If I know my own heart, I humbly say with Paul, "I am ready." Yes, I am willing for God to use me in any way He sees fit. I would not deliberately withhold from Him anything or any service which He requires of me. For many years my chiefest joy and my deepest satisfaction has been to find out God's will for me and then do my best to carry out His will. I well know that all too often I have come short and failed. On many occasions, I am sure, the Master must have been disappointed in me because of my lack of understanding and my poor performance. But I think He knew that in my heart was the readiness to do His will. Perhaps that is why His patience and forgiving mercy and sustaining grace have been granted unto me so generously and unfailingly. If I know anything, I know that I want Christ to have His way with me in this world and in the world to come.

And what about you, dear friends, who are not professed Christians, who have never accepted and confessed Christ as Saviour, Lord and Master? No doubt you have thought, and even intended, that some day you would accept and confess and follow Christ. But thus far you have postponed the decision, you have put the matter off, you have procrastinated, you have said, "I'll wait for a more convenient season." Are you ready now to end your delay, your indecision, your procrastination, your pushing of Christ aside, your neglect of your own soul's salvation? Are you ready to give the "yes" of your mind, your heart and your will to Christ? Without Christ as your Saviour and Lord you are not ready to live, you are not ready to die, and certainly you are not ready to stand before the judgment bar of God. If you would be ready to make the most of this life and the life to come, then I beseech you to accept and confess Christ now and begin from this hour to follow and obey and serve and love Him forever. Then, indeed, will you be able to say with Paul, "I am ready."

SERMON XIV

Christian Assurance

S E R M O N   X I V

Christian Assurance

~~~~~~

I know whom I have believed, and am persuaded that He is able to keep that which I have committed unto Him against that day.

II TIMOTHY 1:12

IF YOU were asked to name the three things of this world that most baffle and perplex the children of men, would they not be these three—sin, sorrow, death? I am sure that would be our answer. Wherever we turn, in whatever land we may be, with whatever class or condition we may associate, we would put sin and sorrow and death as the three major problems confronting mankind.

Fortunately for us, the Bible has the sure word of truth concerning these three most terrible matters. Paul states the word of certainty concerning each of them. Let me give three of his statements:

"I know whom I have believed, and am persuaded that He is able to keep that which I have committed unto Him against that day." "We know that all things work together for good to them that love God, to them who are called according to His purpose." "And we know that if this earthly house, this tabernacle of dust, is destroyed, we will have a building from God, a house not made with hands, eternal in the heavens."

Certainly of the very matters that most baffle and perplex the children of men, God's word speaks with the note of certainty. Sin, that awful plague of human life! Over against the fact of sin there is set an almighty and all-sufficient Saviour. Sorrow, the guest that walks in every home and is

in every life! Over against that fact the Bible sets an over-
ruling heavenly Father, who for His children makes every
conceivable sorrow to come out for His child's good. And
death, that most terrible mystery of all, that grim sarcasm
of human life! Over against that fact is set a more glorious
fact; namely, that death is but the dusky gateway through
which Christ's believing child passes through to the eternal
city, to be at home forever with God.

These are the things that men and women want to know.
They want to know about sin and its deliverance, about
sorrow and its surcease, about death and its conqueror; and
the Bible speaks with absolute certainty concerning these
three great mysteries and trials of the human heart.

It is a wonderfully interesting study to take the concordance
to your Bible and see with what certainty the Bible speaks on
the matters that need elucidation and clearness and positiveness; how it wastes no time on the speculative and the theo-
retical and the unimportant. But on matters that need dogmatism and certainty the Bible is as clear as the sun in its
meridian brilliance. It is an interesting study to follow Paul
as he deals with these great facts and problems of human life.
All the verses I have read to you are the statements of Paul.
There were things that he did not presume to pass upon, that
he was not dogmatic upon; but about these serious things
on which all normal-minded people want information—sin,
sorrow and death—about them Paul spoke with certainty.

Paul was certain, first of all, that he had a Saviour, for he
had seen Him. "I know whom I have believed, and am persuaded that He is able to keep that which I have committed
unto Him against that day." Paul was certain that he had a
Saviour from sin. In Paul's day, just as in this day, sin was
rampant everywhere. One dismal, obstrusive fact on every
side, in Paul's life and in your life and mine, is the devas-
tating power of sin. Account of its rule runs through the
Bible from the first chapters of Genesis to the last chapters

in Revelation, where the golden gateway of the New Jerusalem is for a moment opened to our view. Through the Bible there runs the awful problem and mystery of sin. But over against that fact Paul set an almighty and all-sufficient Saviour.

Sin, in Paul's day, reigned—so he tells us—unto death. The past was beclouded by sin and the present was marked and marred by sin; with thought of the future were the spectres, the apprehensions, and the apparitions of sin. Oh, Paul didn't gloss over sin! Nor does the Bible gloss over sin. The one dismal fact that flashes forth constantly from the pages of God's Book is the fact of sin. All the havoc of earth, all the diseases of the race, all the machinations that have come to perplex the world follow in the wake of sin. Paul knew it. Read the first chapter of Romans, and the soul turns away with a sinking heart, sickened indescribably, for there the horror of sin is poured out. But Paul stopped not then. Over against the fact of sin he set the Saviour, the all-sufficient Saviour, the Saviour who could shake the fetters of sin from every soul. His blood could cleanse the sinner of every sin. Paul speaks the word of certainty. "I am the chief sinner," says he. "My life was marred and distorted and blackened by sin. I was the chief sinner of all men." He had been arrogant, presumptuous, domineering, tyrannical, self-centered, self-willed and self-righteous—all that, and much more, was Saul of Tarsus. But the Apostle Paul says: "He saved me. I know whom I have believed." Now, that is what *we* want to know.

To be sure, Paul saw the mysteries that attached to sin. The problem of evil, the mystery of evil, the why and how sin came is as old as the world. But he didn't stop to gloss over sin and speculate upon it. Paul saw Him who came in human flesh and took man's place—the innocent for the guilty—that divine justice might be satisfied. Paul saw Him on the Damascus road; and from that time he went up and down the earth, from one land to another, scorning ease—mocking and smiting ease at every hour— to say to men everywhere: "Gripped and manacled as you are by sin, I present you a Saviour, one who is almighty and all-sufficient. No guess-work, no speculation, no theorizing, no fancying, no star-gazing, no delaying. I was a sinner. Sin had mastery over me. I was the chief of sinners, when One stood forth who said, 'I will give you mastery over sin if you will take me to be your sin-bearer, your redeemer.' I took Him. I know whom I have believed. I know about it."

Oh, brethren, what might, what power there is in that kind of witness concerning Christ!

Paul said: "Putting everything human aside, all of it is as a broken reed, I have found a Saviour who has broken the fetters, who has set me free, who has given peace to my mind, who has given rest to my soul. I know, I know!"

The world cares and is weary and dies for that positive knowledge. A thousand and one fads outcrop in our time, grow up in a night, catch the unwary and the uninformed, because they seem to offer a measure of certainty. Alas, their seeming certainty is as quicksand! They have no Rock of Ages on which one may stand secure for time and eternity.

Well did the pastor of Tremont Temple, in Boston, say that the most respectable religion in Boston is a religion that laughs at the fact of sin and the fact of an atoning Saviour. He indicated that the most respectable religion in Boston teaches that though men get drunk and kill and lie; yet, to this religion, there is nothing wrong anywhere, except that men just have a bad thought or a nightmare.

Paul was not so deluded. He was the chief sinner of the world. "I was the chief of sinners," he said, "but I met One who on Golgotha's hill washed away my sins in His own blood from five great gaping wounds. My sins were atoned for by His shed blood. I met Him and put my life in His hands and He set me free."

Any religion that minimizes sin is from the darkness of the pit and is born of the evil one. Sin reigns everywhere. Men under the power of sin reach the conclusion often that there is no difference between right and wrong, and right is thrown to the wind and the heart is mastered by the deceiver of men. Paul said: "My certainty comes from personal contact with the Son of God. I know whom I have believed. He stood forth as a burden-bearer for the sinner, the deliverer of the sinner. He stood forth as the redeemer. I know about Him! I know about Him! He declared Himself before me. I received Him as my Saviour and found that He had power to break the fetters of sin and relieve the accusing conscience."

That is what we want. That is what the hungry world needs. Deep down in the human heart—whatever its money, its social distinctions, its environment—down in the human heart is a soul which longs for pardon, peace and power which Christ alone can give. How supremely important therefore it is that Christ Jesus, God's Son, be presented to such soul as the one and only Saviour who is sufficient to save from the thraldom, the doom, the power of sin and Satan!

Nor did Paul stop at that. He said: "I am persuaded that this Saviour whom I have believed is able to keep that which I have committed unto Him against that day." The most glorious doctrine in all the world is Christ's ability to keep his deserving child. Not that Paul was able. Not that you and I are able. Satan is more than a match for any saint that ever lived unless Christ helps and protects that saint. Paul says: "Christ is able to keep that which I have committed unto Him against that day." Again he says: "I am persuaded that neither death, nor angels, nor principalities, nor powers, nor things present, nor things to come, nor height, nor depth, nor any creature shall be able to separate us from the love of God, which is in Christ Jesus, our Lord."

What a note of certainty you find where you most need it! "Is this certainty yours?" The hungry world wants to know.

Is this certainty yours? Down in the heart are you able to say with the Apostle of all the ages: "I have found one who has given peace; a person, not a theory, not a fancy, not a figment of the imagination; a person real like mother, on whose breast I have leaned sobbing many times because of my unworthiness, broken because of my sin. I have found a person, and that person has forgiven me and comforted me and put some reigning principle in my life that makes me hate sin and love righteousness"—are you able to say that?

A lady once asked that great scientist, Sir James Simpson of Edinburgh, the great physician who discovered chloroform and applied it to the relief of suffering humanity, "Doctor, you have made many discoveries; what do you count your greatest?" "Madam," said the great scientist, as his eyes filled with tears, "incomparably the greatest discovery I have ever made is that Jesus Christ has saved me, a poor sinner." Have you made that discovery? All the figments of the imagination, all your dreams and theories and all your laughing at sin shall at last leave you in midstream, helpless and appalled. You are a sinner condemned under the law of Almighty God. Your sin must perish in you or in one who stands for you. Christ stands for you, the just for the unjust.

That is the first great certainty. Paul said: "I well know that all things work together for good to them that love God." No guesswork there, no speculation. Paul was a man of sorrows, a man who suffered great tribulations and much persecution. From the day of his conversion on the road to Damascus until the old man's head was chopped from his shoulders, he was a man of sorrow. He said: "I suffer the loss of all things for my religion. My friends, my position, my inheritance, my standing among the Jews—all things I lost for my religion. I have had denials from friends and foes. I have had weariness and affliction, despairing sometimes almost of any hope to live. Yet it will all work out all right, for my Father knows and my Father cares and my Father rules." Isn't that a glorious doctrine for the Christian?

I stood beside a mother in this city as she gave her child to the grave. "I know it is right," she said between her sobs. "He doeth all things well." There is the victory of faith. We know that all things work together for good to them that love God. He can and will transform all of life's storms and sorrows into blessings for the good of his child. He delights to come along with every black-gowned messenger and Himself sanctify the grief of the message to the good of his child. Isn't that a glorious truth?

The Christian business man, beaten and driven, going here and there in the blinding storm, knows what the un-Christian man cannot know. He says: "God reigns and rules the world, and Him can I trust." He does not understand it. He is all perplexed and baffled, tears come like copious showers, but above the din and confusion and noise of the world he says: "My Father knows and cares, and somehow will manage all well." Isn't that the thing that men want to know? "We know that all things work together for good to them that love God." Mystery everywhere, baffling, perplexing mystery; and the sobs of the world and the lamentations of the weary come to appall us, but the Christian says: "It will come out all right. My father knows and cares. Not even a sparrow falls but that He knows. I had rather walk in the dark with Him than to walk by myself in the light. It will come out all right."

I have seen the tear-filled eyes as He chastened men and women now looking into my face, and through their suffering and tears and sorrow, with chastened heart, they said and said again: "It will come out all right. He reigns and rules and overrules. It will work out all right, because I am God's child."

There is another mystery—that grim sarcasm which is death. "It is appointed unto man once to die." It is something that all of us know. There is no discharge from this war. Then, is there light? Right where we want it most, light flashes forth like the great sun at noonday. "We know that if this earthly tabernacle be destroyed, we shall have a house not made with hands, eternal in the heavens."

Plato and Socrates speculated and theorized about the hereafter, but spoke no word of certainty about it. All can merely speculate who leave out the word of God; all are adrift who put the Bible behind them.

We know that, if this mortal body in which lives the real person—that which thinks and wills and loves—if this body is destroyed, as destroyed it will be, the real person has a building of God, a house not made by hands, eternal in the heavens. When you close those poor tired eyes of yours and fold those wearied hands together for the last sleep, the spirit, liberated and disentangled, in one moment is in the building of God, the house of many mansions, the Father's own house for his children. Isn't that what we want to know? Paul says all it means is to move out of he body, vacate the old, and the spirit is at once at home in the Father's house. And in the fullness of God's purpose He brings that body up, for Satan shall not have even the body. Nor will Christ's great work be done until these old, scarred bodies are raised from the grave, as raised they will be, when Christ does His work of resurrection. The old body returns to dust, but the spirit promptly goes on to be at home with the Lord.

Oh, we don't ask Job's question now — "Shall man live again?" Of that we no more doubt than we doubt our presence in this building this morning. Isn't that the word we want to know? Oh, Death, thou mystery of life and love and joy; oh, Death, thou dost not have the victory! Christ was dead and then was alive. He explored every dark cavern in the chamber of death. Not one place in all that dark chamber did Christ fail to explore, and Christ has hanging to his girdle the keys of death and the world invisible. By Him our bodies will be raised up from the dust and, being glorified, they will be at home when the vast mansion is at last finished for his children.

These are the certainties for men. There was never anything more tragic in this world than for men to try to laugh sin out of court—for men to gloss over sin. Sin would kill God if it could. Sin has lighted every fire in hell; it has wrought every havoc. Every man has the awful virus in his body. Laughing at it, laughing at it but makes the tragedy a thousand times worse, and by adding insult to injury makes destruction more sure.

God recognizes that man is a sinner, and therefore God provides for the sinner a Saviour. That Saviour we must accept and follow all the way, through all the days and through all the circumstances of life. He can and will guide us aright. He will empower us to know and do God's will. He will be with us always, in life, in death and beyond forever. He will guide us home to the Father's house of many mansions. Therefore, like Paul, we can commit to Him our all—our salvation, our soul's destiny, our every interest in this life and for the life to come. He is able! He is able to save unto the uttermost and He is able to keep all that which we commit unto Him.

Oh, men and women, I dare say that deep down in the heart of every one of you there is the desire to be conqueror over sin, sorrow and death. You need an all-powerful helper, a sin-bearer, an all-sufficient Saviour, One in whom you can put your full trust, One on whom you can utterly rely. The One you need is Jesus, the Christ, the Son of God, the Saviour of the world. I can and do say with Paul, "I know Him whom I have believed, and am persuaded that He is able to keep that which I have committed unto Him against that great day." I know that He is the adequate Saviour because He has saved me and given unto me the assurance of eternal life—

not because of any merits that were found in me, a poor and needy sinner, but it was all of grace. I can never cease to marvel that I was an object of His loving grace and that He bore my sins in His own body upon the tree, that I, having died unto sins, might live unto righteousness. By His grace, through faith, we are saved. By His stripes we are healed.

This blessed Saviour, concerning whom my heart gladly gives its witness, not only saves from the guilt and doom of sin but He also gives garlands for ashes, the oil of joy for mourning, and garments of praise for the spirit of heaviness. He enables His friends to smile through their tears, to see and feel the silver linings beyond the clouds of day and the stars of hope in the darkest night. His comforting word is: "Be of good cheer; I have overcome the world."

And then there is the glorious truth that the Christian may have full assurance and strong confidence as he faces the last enemy, which is death. Christ gives the victory there also. To His friends He says, "Because I live, you shall live also." He met death and the grave, and came forth conqueror. This fact enables the Christian to shout, "O death, where is thy sting? O grave, where is thy victory?" Through Christ the victory is given over sin and sorrow and death. In Him is life and from Him the Christian receives life eternal, blessed for evermore. The Christian's hope for time and eternity rests upon a sure foundation. That is why he is justified in singing:

> My hope is built on nothing less
> Than Jesus' blood and righteousness.
> I dare not trust the sweetest frame,
> But wholly lean on Jesus' name.

Are you a Christian? Throw to the winds all else but Jesus, and having Him, you have the victory over sin and sorrow and death. Then you can join with Paul in saying:

"I know whom I have believed, and am persuaded that He is able to keep that which I have committed unto Him against that day." And you can also say: "I know that all things work together for good to them that love God, to them who are called according to His purpose." And again you can say with Paul: "I shall have a building from God, a house not made with hands, eternal in the heavens."

O men and women, believe on Christ today and trust Him forever!